Cram101 Textbook Outlines to accompany:

Brief Introduction to Fluid Mechanics

Donald F. Young, Bruce Roy Munson, Theodore H. Okiishi, 4th Edition

A Cram101 Inc. publication (c) 2010.

Cram101 Textbook Outlines and Cram101.com are Cram101 Inc. publications and services. All notes, highlights, reviews, and practice tests are written and prepared by Cram101, all rights reserved.

PRACTICE EXAMS.

Get all of the self-teaching practice exams for each chapter of this textbook at **www.Cram101.com** and ace the tests. Here is an example:

Chapter 1

Brief Introduction to Fluid Mechanics
Donald F. Young, Bruce Roy Munson, Theodore H. Okiishi, 4th Edition,
All Material Written and Prepared by Cram101

I WANT A BETTER GRADE.   Items 1 - 50 of 100.

1. In physics and fluid mechanics, a _____ is that layer of fluid in the immediate vicinity of a bounding surface. In the Earth"s atmosphere, the planetary _____ is the air layer near the ground affected by diurnal heat, moisture or momentum transfer to or from the surface. On an aircraft wing the _____ is the part of the flow close to the wing.

   - Boundary layer
   - Back pressure
   - Balance bicycle
   - Banana Doughnut theory

2. A _____ is a substance that continually deforms (flows) under an applied shear stress. All gases are _____s, but not all liquids are _____s. Fluids are a subset of the phases of matter and include liquids, gases, plasmas and, to some extent, plastic solids.

   - Fluid
   - Facility for Rare Isotopes Beams
   - Factor of safety
   - Factorials

3. _____ is the study of the flow of matter: mainly liquids but also soft solids or solids under conditions in which they flow rather than deform elastically. It applies to substances which have a complex structure, including muds, sludges, suspensions, polymers, many foods, bodily fluids, and other biological materials. The flow of these substances cannot be characterized by a single value of viscosity - instead the viscosity changes due to other factors.

   - Rheology
   - Rabi cycle
   - Rabi frequency
   - Rabi problem

You get a 50% discount for the online exams. Go to **Cram101.com**, click Sign Up at the top of the screen, and enter DK73DW6263 in the promo code box on the registration screen. Access to Cram101.com is $4.95 per month, cancel at any time.

With Cram101.com online, you also have access to extensive reference material.

You will nail those essays and papers. Here is an example from a Cram101 Biology text:

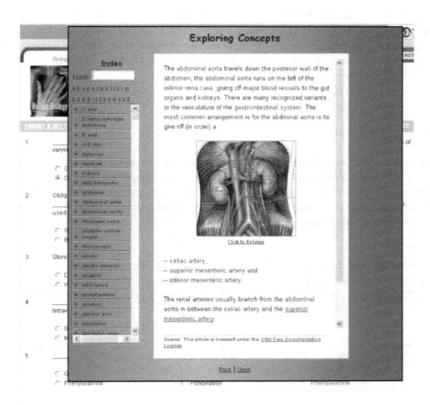

Visit **www.Cram101.com**, click Sign Up at the top of the screen, and enter DK73DW6263 in the promo code box on the registration screen. Access to www.Cram101.com is normally $9.95 per month, but because you have purchased this book, your access fee is only $4.95 per month, cancel at any time. Sign up and stop highlighting textbooks forever.

Learning System

Cram101 Textbook Outlines is a learning system. The notes in this book are the highlights of your textbook, you will never have to highlight a book again.

How to use this book. Take this book to class, it is your notebook for the lecture. The notes and highlights on the left hand side of the pages follow the outline and order of the textbook. All you have to do is follow along while your instructor presents the lecture. Circle the items emphasized in class and add other important information on the right side. With Cram101 Textbook Outlines you'll spend less time writing and more time listening. Learning becomes more efficient.

Cram101.com Online

Increase your studying efficiency by using Cram101.com's practice tests and online reference material. It is the perfect complement to Cram101 Textbook Outlines. Use self-teaching matching tests or simulate in-class testing with comprehensive multiple choice tests, or simply use Cram's true and false tests for quick review. Cram101.com even allows you to enter your in-class notes for an integrated studying format combining the textbook notes with your class notes.

Visit **www.Cram101.com**, click Sign Up at the top of the screen, and enter **DK73DW6263** in the promo code box on the registration screen. Access to www.Cram101.com is normally $9.95 per month, but because you have purchased this book, your access fee is only $4.95 per month. Sign up and stop highlighting textbooks forever.

Copyright © 2010 by Cram101, Inc. All rights reserved. "Cram101"® and "Never Highlight a Book Again!"® are registered trademarks of Cram101, Inc. ISBN(s): 9781428850767. EDE-1.2009129

Brief Introduction to Fluid Mechanics
Donald F. Young, Bruce Roy Munson, Theodore H. Okiishi, 4th

CONTENTS

1. INTRODUCTION 2
2. FLUID STATICS 18
3. ELEMENTARY FLUID DYNAMICS-THE BERNOULLI EQUATION 30
4. FLUID KINEMATICS 40
5. FINITE CONTROL VOLUME ANALYSIS 44
6. DIFFERENTIAL ANALYSIS OF FLUID FLOW 60
7. SIMILITUDE, DIMENSIONAL ANALYSIS, AND MODELING 72
8. VISCOUS FLOW IN PIPES 78
9. FLOW OVER IMMERSED BODIES 88
10. OPEN-CHANNEL FLOW 102
11. TURBOMACHINES 110

Chapter 1. INTRODUCTION

Boundary layer
In physics and fluid mechanics, a Boundary layer is that layer of fluid in the immediate vicinity of a bounding surface. In the Earth"s atmosphere, the planetary Boundary layer is the air layer near the ground affected by diurnal heat, moisture or momentum transfer to or from the surface. On an aircraft wing the Boundary layer is the part of the flow close to the wing.

Fluid
A Fluid is a substance that continually deforms (flows) under an applied shear stress. All gases are Fluids, but not all liquids are Fluids. Fluids are a subset of the phases of matter and include liquids, gases, plasmas and, to some extent, plastic solids.

Rheology
Rheology is the study of the flow of matter: mainly liquids but also soft solids or solids under conditions in which they flow rather than deform elastically. It applies to substances which have a complex structure, including muds, sludges, suspensions, polymers, many foods, bodily fluids, and other biological materials. The flow of these substances cannot be characterized by a single value of viscosity - instead the viscosity changes due to other factors.

Atmosphere
An Atmosphere is a layer of gases that may surround a material body of sufficient mass, by the gravity of the body, and are retained for a longer duration if gravity is high and the Atmosphere"s temperature is low. Some planets consist mainly of various gases, but only their outer layer is their Atmosphere .
The term stellar Atmosphere describes the outer region of a star, and typically includes the portion starting from the opaque photosphere outwards.

Acceleration
Acceleration is the rate of change of velocity. At any point on a trajectory, the magnitude of the Acceleration is given by the rate of change of velocity in both magnitude and direction at that point. The true Acceleration at time t is found in the limit as time interval $\Delta t \to 0$. Components of Acceleration for a planar curved motion.

Kilogram
The Kilogram (symbol: kg) is the base unit of mass in the International System of Units . The Kilogram is defined as being equal to the mass of the International Prototype Kilogram , which is almost exactly equal to the mass of one liter of water. It is the only SI base unit with an SI prefix as part of its name.

Mass
In physics, Mass commonly refers to any of three properties of matter, which have been shown experimentally to be equivalent: inertial Mass, active gravitational Mass and passive gravitational Mass. In everyday usage, Mass is often taken to mean weight, but care should be taken to distinguish between the two terms in scientific use, as they actually refer to different properties.
The inertial Mass of an object determines its acceleration in the presence of an applied force.

Pound
The pound -mass (abbreviation: lb, lbm, or) is a unit of mass used in the imperial, United States customary and other systems of measurement. A number of different definitions have been used, the most common today being the international avoirdupois pound of exactly 0.453 592 37 kilogram.
The word pound comes from the Latin word pondus meaning "weight". The abbreviation lb comes from the Latin word libra, meaning "scales, balances", which also described a Roman unit similar to the pound .

Pound-force
The pound-force or simply pound (abbreviations: lb, lbf, or lb_f) is a unit of force.

{ # Chapter 1. INTRODUCTION

Chapter 1. INTRODUCTION

	The pound-force is approximately equal to the gravitational force exerted on a mass of one avoirdupois pound on the surface of Earth. Since the 18th century, the unit has been used in low-precision measurements, for which small changes in Earth"s gravity can safely be neglected.
Weber number	The Weber number is a dimensionless number in fluid mechanics that is often useful in analysing fluid flows where there is an interface between two different fluids, especially for multiphase flows with strongly curved surfaces. It can be thought of as a measure of the relative importance of the fluid"s inertia compared to its surface tension. The quantity is useful in analyzing thin film flows and the formation of droplets and bubbles. It is named after Moritz Weber (1871-1951) and may be written as: $$We = \frac{\rho v^2 l}{\sigma}$$ where · ρ is the density of the fluid. · v is its velocity. · l is its characteristic length, typically the droplet diameter. · σ is the surface tension.
Power	In physics, power is the rate at which work is performed or energy is converted. It is an energy per unit of time. As a rate of change of work done or the energy of a subsystem, power is $$P = \frac{W}{t}$$ where P is power, W is work and t is time.
Density	The Density of a material is defined as its mass per unit volume. The symbol of Density is ρ. Mathematically: $$\rho = \frac{m}{V}$$ where: ρ is the Density, m is the mass, V is the volume.
Fluid dynamics	In physics, Fluid dynamics is a sub-discipline of fluid mechanics that deals with fluid flow--the natural science of fluids (liquids and gases) in motion. It has several subdisciplines itself, including aerodynamics (the study of air and other gases in motion) and hydrodynamics (the study of liquids in motion). Fluid dynamics has a wide range of applications, including calculating forces and moments on aircraft, determining the mass flow rate of petroleum through pipelines, predicting weather patterns, understanding nebulae in interstellar space and reportedly modeling fission weapon detonation.

Chapter 1. INTRODUCTION

Chapter 1. INTRODUCTION

Fluid statics Fluid statics is the science of fluids at rest, and is a sub-field within fluid mechanics. The term usually refers to the mathematical treatment of the subject. It embraces the study of the conditions under which fluids are at rest in stable equilibrium.

Static Statics is the branch of mechanics concerned with the analysis of loads (force, torque/moment) on physical systems in Static equilibrium, that is, in a state where the relative positions of subsystems do not vary over time, the system is either at rest, or its center of mass moves at constant velocity. The study of moving bodies is known as dynamics.

Volume The density of an object is defined as mass per unit volume. The inverse of density is specific volume which is defined as volume divided by mass.

volume and capacity are sometimes distinguished, with capacity being used for how much a container can hold (with contents measured commonly in liters or its derived units), and volume being how much space an object displaces (commonly measured in cubic meters or its derived units).

Bulk modulus The Bulk modulus (K) of a substance measures the substance"s resistance to uniform compression. It is defined as the pressure increase needed to cause a given relative decrease in volume. Its base unit is Pascal.

Equation of state
$$p = \rho RT + \left(B_0 RT - A_0 - \frac{C_0}{T^2} + \frac{D_0}{T^3} - \frac{E_0}{T^4}\right)\rho^2 + \left(bRT - a - \frac{d}{T}\right)\rho^3 + \alpha\left(a + \frac{d}{T}\right)\rho^6 + \frac{c\rho^3}{T^2}\left(1 + \gamma\rho^2\right)\exp\left(-\gamma\rho^2\right)$$

where
p = pressure
ρ = the molar density
Values of the various parameters for 15 substances can be found in:
K.E. Starling, Fluid Properties for Light Petroleum Systems. Gulf Publishing Company (1973).
When considering water under very high pressures (typical applications are underwater nuclear explosions, sonic shock lithotripsy, and sonoluminescence) the stiffened Equation of state is often used:

$$p = \rho(\gamma - 1)e - \gamma p^0$$

where e is the internal energy per unit mass, γ is an empirically determined constant typically taken to be about 6.1, and p^0 is another constant, representing the molecular attraction between water molecules.

Gas constant The Gas constant (also known as the molar, universal, or ideal Gas constant, denoted by the symbol R or R) is a physical constant which is featured in a large number of fundamental equations in the physical sciences, such as the ideal gas law and the Nernst equation. It is equivalent to the Boltzmann constant, but expressed in units of energy (i.e. the pressure-volume product) per kelvin per mole (rather than energy per kelvin per particle).
Its value is

Chapter 1. INTRODUCTION

Chapter 1. INTRODUCTION

$$R = 8.314472(15)\ \frac{\text{J}}{\text{K mol}}.$$

The two digits in parentheses are the uncertainty (standard deviation) in the last two digits of the value.

Ideal gas law	The Ideal gas law is the equation of state of a hypothetical ideal gas. It is a good approximation to the behavior of many gases under many conditions, although it has several limitations. It was first stated by Émile Clapeyron in 1834 as a combination of Boyle"s law and Charles"s law.
Physical properties	A physical property is any aspect of an object or substance that can be measured or perceived without changing its identity. Physical properties can be intensive or extensive. An intensive property does not depend on the size or amount of matter in the object, while an extensive property does.
Surface tension	Surface tension is a property of the surface of a liquid. It is what causes the surface portion of liquid to be attracted to another surface, such as that of another portion of liquid (as in connecting bits of water or as in a drop of mercury that forms a cohesive ball). Applying Newtonian physics to the forces that arise due to Surface tension accurately predicts many liquid behaviors that are so commonplace that most people take them for granted.
Vapor	A vapor (American spelling) or vapour is a substance in the gas phase at a temperature lower than its critical temperature. This means that the vapor can be condensed to a liquid or to a solid by increasing its pressure, without reducing the temperature. For example, water has a critical temperature of 374°C (or 647 K) which is the highest temperature at which liquid water can exist.
Vapor pressure	Vapor pressure or equilibrium Vapor pressure is the pressure of a vapor in thermodynamic equilibrium with its condensed phases in a closed container. All liquids and solids have a tendency to evaporate into a gaseous form, and all gases have a tendency to condense back to their liquid or solid form. The equilibrium Vapor pressure is an indication of a liquid"s evaporation rate.
Viscosity	Viscosity is a measure of the resistance of a fluid which is being deformed by either shear stress or extensional stress. In everyday terms (and for fluids only), Viscosity is "thickness." Thus, water is "thin," having a lower Viscosity, while honey is "thick," having a higher Viscosity. Viscosity describes a fluid"s internal resistance to flow and may be thought of as a measure of fluid friction.
Velocity	In physics, velocity is the rate of change of position. It is a vector physical quantity; both speed and direction are required to define it. In the SI (metric) system, it is measured in meters per second: (m/s) or ms^{-1}.
Vortex ring toy	A Vortex ring toy generates vortex rings -- rolling donut-shapes of fluid -- which move through the fluid (most often air, and). A smoke ring is a common example of a vortex ring. Because of the way they rotate, a vortex ring can hold itself together and travel for quite a distance.

Chapter 1. INTRODUCTION

Chapter 1. INTRODUCTION

No-slip condition

In fluid dynamics, the No-slip condition for viscous fluid states that at a solid boundary, the fluid will have zero velocity relative to the boundary.

The fluid velocity at all fluid-solid boundaries is equal to that of the solid boundary. Conceptually, one can think of the outermost molecules of fluid as stuck to the surfaces past which it flows.

Force

In physics, a Force has the capacity to change the motion of a free body or cause stress in a fixed body. It can also be described by intuitive concepts such as a push or pull that can cause an object with mass to change its velocity, i.e., to accelerate, or which can cause a flexible object to deform. Force has both magnitude and direction, making it a vector quantity.

Newtonian fluid

A Newtonian fluid is a fluid whose stress versus strain rate curve is linear and passes through the origin. The constant of proportionality is known as the viscosity.

A simple equation to describe Newtonian fluid behaviour is

$$\tau = \mu \frac{du}{dy}$$

where

τ is the shear stress exerted by the fluid ("drag") [Pa]

μ is the fluid viscosity - a constant of proportionality [Pa·s]

$\frac{du}{dy}$ is the velocity gradient perpendicular to the direction of shear [s^{-1}]

In common terms, this means the fluid continues to flow, regardless of the forces acting on it.

Non-Newtonian fluid

A Non-Newtonian fluid is a fluid whose flow properties are not described by a single constant value of viscosity. Many polymer solutions and molten polymers are Non-Newtonian fluids, as are many commonly found substances such as ketchup, starch suspensions, paint, blood and shampoo. In a Newtonian fluid, the relation between the shear stress and the strain rate is linear (and if one were to plot this relationship, it would pass through the origin), the constant of proportionality being the coefficient of viscosity.

Shearing

Shearing in continuum mechanics refers to the occurrence of a shear strain, which is a deformation of a material substance in which parallel internal surfaces slide past one another. It is induced by a shear stress in the material. Shear strain is distinguished from volumetric strain, the change in a material"s volume in response to stress.

Strain rate

Strain rate, with regards to materials science, is the change in strain over the change in time and is denoted as $\dot{\varepsilon}$.

$\dot{\varepsilon} = \delta\varepsilon/\delta t$ Strain rate is rate of deformation

We have

$$\dot{\varepsilon} = \delta\varepsilon/\delta t = \frac{1}{\ell_0}\frac{d\ell}{dt} = \frac{v}{\ell_0}$$

where ℓ_0 is the original length and v is the speed of deformation.

Chapter 1. INTRODUCTION

Chapter 1. INTRODUCTION

	In a Newtonian fluid, the relation between the shear stress and the rate of strain is linear, the constant of proportionality being the coefficient of viscosity.
Stress	In linguistics, stress is the relative emphasis that may be given to certain syllables in a word. The term is also used for similar patterns of phonetic prominence inside syllables. The word accent is sometimes also used with this sense.
Reynolds number	In fluid mechanics, the Reynolds number Re is a dimensionless number that gives a measure of the ratio of inertial forces (ρV^2) to viscous forces $\left(\dfrac{\mu V}{L}\right)$ and consequently quantifies the relative importance of these two types of forces for given flow conditions. The Reynolds number is named after Osborne Reynolds (1842-1912), who introduced its use in 1883. Reynolds numbers frequently arise when performing dimensional analysis of fluid dynamics problems, and as such can be used to determine dynamic similitude between different experimental cases. They are also used to characterize different flow regimes, such as laminar or turbulent flow: laminar flow occurs at low Reynolds numbers, where viscous forces are dominant, and is characterized by smooth, constant fluid motion, while turbulent flow occurs at high Reynolds numbers and is dominated by inertial forces, which tend to produce random eddies, vortices and other flow instabilities.
Elastic modulus	An Elastic modulus, is the mathematical description of an object or substance"s tendency to be deformed elastically (i.e., non-permanently) when a force is applied to it. The Elastic modulus of an object is defined as the slope of its stress-strain curve in the elastic deformation region: $$\lambda \stackrel{\text{def}}{=} \frac{\text{stress}}{\text{strain}}$$ where λ (lambda) is the Elastic modulus; *stress* is the force causing the deformation divided by the area to which the force is applied; and *strain* is the ratio of the change caused by the stress to the original state of the object. If stress is measured in pascals, since strain is a unitless ratio, then the units of λ are pascals as well.
Isothermal	An isothermal process is a change of a system, in which the temperature remains constant: ΔT = 0. This typically occurs when a system is in contact with an outside thermal reservoir (heat bath), and the change occurs slowly enough to allow the system to continually adjust to the temperature of the reservoir through heat exchange. An alternative special case in which a system exchanges no heat with its surroundings (Q = 0) is called an adiabatic process. In other words, in an isothermal process, the value ΔT = 0 but Q ≠ 0, while in an adiabatic process, ΔT ≠ 0 but Q = 0. Several isotherms of an ideal gas on a p-V diagram For the special case of a gas to which Boyle"s law applies, the product pV is a constant if the gas is kept at isothermal conditions.

Chapter 1. INTRODUCTION

Chapter 1. INTRODUCTION

Acoustic	Acoustic or sonic lubrication occurs when sound (measurable in a vacuum by placing a microphone on one element of the sliding system) permits vibration to introduce separation between the sliding faces. This could happen between two plates or between a series of particles. The frequency of sound required to induce optimal vibration, and thus cause sonic lubrication, varies with the size of the particles (high frequencies will have the desired, or undesired, effect on sand and lower frequencies will have this effect on boulders).
Sound	Sound is a travelling wave which is an oscillation of pressure transmitted through a solid, liquid, composed of frequencies within the range of hearing and of a level sufficiently strong to be heard, or the sensation stimulated in organs of hearing by such vibrations. Human ear
For humans, hearing is normally limited to frequencies between about 12 Hz and 20,000 Hz (20 kHz), although these limits are not definite. The upper limit generally decreases with age.
Cavitation	Cavitation is the formation of vapour bubbles of a flowing liquid in a region where the pressure of the liquid falls below its vapor pressure. Cavitation is usually divided into two classes of behavior: inertial (or transient) Cavitation, and noninertial Cavitation. Inertial Cavitation is the process where a void or bubble in a liquid rapidly collapses, producing a shock wave.
Angle of attack	Angle of attack is a term used in fluid dynamics to describe the angle between a reference line on a lifting body and the vector representing the relative motion between the lifting body and the fluid through which it is moving. Angle of attack is the angle between the lifting body"s reference line and the oncoming flow.
In aviation, Angle of attack is used to describe the angle between the chord line of the wing of a fixed-wing aircraft and the vector representing the relative motion between the aircraft and the atmosphere.
Capillary action	Capillary action, capillarity, capillary motion, or wicking refers to two phenomena:

· The movement of liquids in thin tubes.

· The flow of liquids through porous media, such as the flow of water through soil.
A common apparatus used to demonstrate the first phenomenon is the capillary tube. When the lower end of a vertical glass tube is placed in a liquid such as water, a concave meniscus forms. |
| Contact angle | The Contact angle is the angle at which a liquid/vapor interface meets the solid surface. The Contact angle is specific for any given system and is determined by the interactions across the three interfaces. Most often the concept is illustrated with a small liquid droplet resting on a flat horizontal solid surface. |
| Froude number | The Froude number is a dimensionless number comparing inertia and gravitational forces. It may be used to quantify the resistance of an object moving through water, and compare objects of different sizes. Named after William Froude, the Froude number is based on his speed/length ratio. |

Chapter 1. INTRODUCTION

Chapter 1. INTRODUCTION

Cylinder | A cylinder is one of the most basic curvilinear geometric shapes, the surface formed by the points at a fixed distance from a given straight line, the axis of the cylinder. The solid enclosed by this surface and by two planes perpendicular to the axis is also called a cylinder. The surface area and the volume of a cylinder have been known since deep antiquity.

Hydraulic head | Hydraulic head or piezometric head is a specific measurement of water pressure above a geodetic datum. It is usually measured as a water surface elevation, expressed in units of length, at the entrance (or bottom) of a piezometer. In an aquifer, it can be calculated from the depth to water in a piezometric well (a specialized water well), and given information of the piezometer"s elevation and screen depth.

Chapter 1. INTRODUCTION

Chapter 2. FLUID STATICS

Fluid	A Fluid is a substance that continually deforms (flows) under an applied shear stress. All gases are Fluids, but not all liquids are Fluids. Fluids are a subset of the phases of matter and include liquids, gases, plasmas and, to some extent, plastic solids.
Fluid statics	Fluid statics is the science of fluids at rest, and is a sub-field within fluid mechanics. The term usually refers to the mathematical treatment of the subject. It embraces the study of the conditions under which fluids are at rest in stable equilibrium.
Static	Statics is the branch of mechanics concerned with the analysis of loads (force, torque/moment) on physical systems in Static equilibrium, that is, in a state where the relative positions of subsystems do not vary over time, the system is either at rest, or its center of mass moves at constant velocity. The study of moving bodies is known as dynamics.
Body force	A Body force is a force that acts throughout the volume of a body. This is in contrast to surface forces, such as shear forces and normal forces, which are exerted only on the surface of the object. Gravity and electromagnetic forces are examples of Body forces.
Force	In physics, a Force has the capacity to change the motion of a free body or cause stress in a fixed body. It can also be described by intuitive concepts such as a push or pull that can cause an object with mass to change its velocity, i.e., to accelerate, or which can cause a flexible object to deform. Force has both magnitude and direction, making it a vector quantity.
Pressure gradient	In atmospheric sciences (meteorology, climatology and related fields), the Pressure gradient (typically of air, more generally of any fluid) is a physical quantity that describes in which direction and at what rate the pressure changes the most rapidly around a particular location. The Pressure gradient is a dimensional quantity expressed in units of pressure per unit length. The SI unit is pascal per metre (Pa/m).
Cylinder	A cylinder is one of the most basic curvilinear geometric shapes, the surface formed by the points at a fixed distance from a given straight line, the axis of the cylinder. The solid enclosed by this surface and by two planes perpendicular to the axis is also called a cylinder. The surface area and the volume of a cylinder have been known since deep antiquity.
Cartesian coordinate system	A Cartesian coordinate system specifies each point uniquely in a plane by a pair of numerical coordinates, which are the signed distances from the point to two fixed perpendicular directed lines, measured in the same unit of length. Each reference line is called a coordinate axis or just axis of the system, and the point where they meet is its origin. The coordinates can also be defined as the positions of the perpendicular projections of the point onto the two axes, expressed as a signed distances from the origin.
Variation	Variation A Variation is a diffrence between species

Chapter 2. FLUID STATICS

Chapter 2. FLUID STATICS

· Biodiversity
· Genetic diversity, differences within a species

· Magnetic Variation, difference between magnetic north and true north, measured as an angle
· Variation (astronomy), any perturbation of the mean motion or orbit of a planet or satellite, particularly of the Moon

· Bounded Variation
· Calculus of Variations, a field of mathematics which deals with functions of functions.
· Permutation

· Coefficient of Variation in statistics, the magnitude of standard deviation relative to the mean.
· Statistical dispersion, a notion of the extent of spread in measurements of a variable, quantified in the variance.

· Variation (music), formal technique where material is altered during repetition
· Variations (album), composed by Andrew Lloyd Webber
· Variation on a theme, in art history

· Variation (ballet), solo dance or dance figure
· Balanchine"s 1947 Theme and Variations (ballet)
· Balanchine"s 1966 Variations (ballet), an earlier version of Variations for Orchestra
· Balanchine"s 1982 Variations for Orchestra, a subsequent revision of Variations

· Variation (game), modifications made to a game by a community of players (as opposed to a central authority)
· Variation (game tree), particular series of moves.
· Variation (linguistics) "

Discharge pressure	Discharge pressure is the pressure generated on the output side of a gas compressor in a refrigeration or air conditioning system. The Discharge pressure is affected by several factors: size and speed of the condenser fan, condition and cleanliness of the condenser coil, and the size of the discharge line. An extremely high Discharge pressure coupled with an extremely low suction pressure is an indicator of a refrigerant restriction.
Pressure coefficient	The pressure coefficient is a dimensionless number which describes the relative pressures throughout a flow field in fluid dynamics. The pressure coefficient is used in aerodynamics and hydrodynamics. Every point in a fluid flow field has its own unique pressure coefficient, C_p.
Pressure head	Pressure head is a term used in fluid mechanics to represent the internal energy of a fluid due to the pressure exerted on its container. It may also be called static Pressure head or simply static head (but not static head pressure). It is mathematically expressed as:

Chapter 2. FLUID STATICS

Chapter 2. FLUID STATICS

$$\psi = \frac{p}{\gamma} = \frac{p}{\rho g}$$

where

ψ is Pressure head (Length, typically in units of m);
p is fluid pressure (Force per unit Area, often as kPa units); and
γ is the specific weight (Weight per unit volume, typically N·m^{-3} units)
ρ is the density of the fluid (Mass per unit volume, typically kg·m^{-3})
g is acceleration due to gravity (rate of change of velocity, given in m·s^{-2})

A Venturi meter with two pressure instruments.

Airfoil	An Airfoil or aerofoil is the shape of a wing or blade (of a propeller, rotor or turbine) or sail as seen in cross-section. An Airfoil-shaped body moved through a fluid produces a force perpendicular to the motion called lift. Subsonic flight Airfoils have a characteristic shape with a rounded leading edge, followed by a sharp trailing edge, often with asymmetric camber.
Atmosphere	An Atmosphere is a layer of gases that may surround a material body of sufficient mass, by the gravity of the body, and are retained for a longer duration if gravity is high and the Atmosphere"s temperature is low. Some planets consist mainly of various gases, but only their outer layer is their Atmosphere. The term stellar Atmosphere describes the outer region of a star, and typically includes the portion starting from the opaque photosphere outwards.
Isothermal	An isothermal process is a change of a system, in which the temperature remains constant: ΔT = 0. This typically occurs when a system is in contact with an outside thermal reservoir (heat bath), and the change occurs slowly enough to allow the system to continually adjust to the temperature of the reservoir through heat exchange. An alternative special case in which a system exchanges no heat with its surroundings (Q = 0) is called an adiabatic process. In other words, in an isothermal process, the value ΔT = 0 but Q ≠ 0, while in an adiabatic process, ΔT ≠ 0 but Q = 0. Several isotherms of an ideal gas on a p-V diagram For the special case of a gas to which Boyle"s law applies, the product pV is a constant if the gas is kept at isothermal conditions.
Suction	Suction is the flow of a fluid into a partial vacuum, which is incorrect since vacuums do not innately attract matter.
Vacuum	In everyday usage, vacuum is a volume of space that is essentially empty of matter, such that its gaseous pressure is much less than atmospheric pressure. The word comes from the Latin term for "empty," but in reality, no volume of space can ever be perfectly empty. Even putting aside the complexities of the quantum vacuum, the classical notion of a perfect vacuum with gaseous pressure of exactly zero is only a philosophical concept and never is observed in practice.

Chapter 2. FLUID STATICS

Chapter 2. FLUID STATICS

Velocity	In physics, velocity is the rate of change of position. It is a vector physical quantity; both speed and direction are required to define it. In the SI (metric) system, it is measured in meters per second: (m/s) or ms^{-1}.
Barometer	A Barometer is an instrument used to measure atmospheric pressure. It can measure the pressure exerted by the atmosphere by using water, air, or mercury. Pressure tendency can forecast short term changes in the weather.
Vapor	A vapor (American spelling) or vapour is a substance in the gas phase at a temperature lower than its critical temperature. This means that the vapor can be condensed to a liquid or to a solid by increasing its pressure, without reducing the temperature. For example, water has a critical temperature of 374°C (or 647 K) which is the highest temperature at which liquid water can exist.
Vapor pressure	Vapor pressure or equilibrium Vapor pressure is the pressure of a vapor in thermodynamic equilibrium with its condensed phases in a closed container. All liquids and solids have a tendency to evaporate into a gaseous form, and all gases have a tendency to condense back to their liquid or solid form. The equilibrium Vapor pressure is an indication of a liquid"s evaporation rate.
Piezometer	A piezometer is a small diameter observation well used to measure the hydraulic head of groundwater in aquifers. Similarly, it may also be a standpipe, tube, vibrating wire piezometer or manometer used to measure the pressure of a fluid at a specific location in a column. piezometers should ideally have a very short screen and filter zone, so that they can represent the hydraulic head at a point in the aquifer.
Transducer	A transducer is a device, electrical, electronic, electro-mechanical, electromagnetic, photonic, that converts one type of energy or physical attribute to another for various purposes including measurement or information transfer (for example: pressure sensors). There are two kinds of transducers: sensors and actuators. A sensor is used to detect a parameter in one form and report it in another form of energy (usually an electrical or digital signal), such as a tachometer.
Expected value	In probability theory and statistics, the expected value (or expectation value, or mean, or first moment) of a random variable is the integral of the random variable with respect to its probability measure. For discrete random variables this is equivalent to the probability-weighted sum of the possible values. For continuous random variables with a density function it is the probability density-weighted integral of the possible values.
First moment of area	The First moment of area is based in the mathematical construct moments in metric spaces, stating that the moment of area equals the summation of area times distance to an axis [Σ(a x d)]. It is a measure of the distribution of the area of a shape in relationship to an axis.

Chapter 2. FLUID STATICS

Chapter 2. FLUID STATICS

	First moment of area is commonly used in engineering applications to determine the centroid of an object or the statical moment of area.
Free surface	In physics a Free surface is the surface of a fluid that is subject to constant perpendicular normal stress and zero parallel shear stress, such as the boundary between two homogenous fluids, for example liquid water and the air in the Earth"s atmosphere. Unlike liquids, gases cannot form a Free surface on their own. A liquid in a gravitational field will form a Free surface if unconfined from above.
Moment of inertia	For the Moment of inertia dealing with bending of a plane, see second moment of area. Moment of inertia, also called mass Moment of inertia or the angular mass, (SI units kgÂ·m^2) is a measure of an object"s resistance to changes in its rotation rate. It is the rotational analog of mass, the inertia of a rigid rotating body with respect to its rotation.
Center of pressure	The Center of pressure is the point on a body where the total sum of the aerodynamic pressure field acts, causing a force and no moment about that point. A stable configuration is not only desirable in sailing, but in aircraft design as well. Aircraft design therefore borrowed the term Center of pressure.
Second moment of area	The Second moment of area, also known as the area moment of inertia or second moment of inertia is a property of a shape that can be used to predict the resistance of beams to bending and deflection. The deflection of a beam under load depends not only on the load, but also on the geometry of the beam"s cross-section. This is why beams with higher area moments of inertia, such as I-beams, are so often seen in building construction as opposed to other beams with the same area.
Metacentric height	The metacentric height (GM) is the distance between the center of gravity of a ship and its metacenter. The GM is used to calculate the stability of a ship and this must be done before it proceeds to sea. The GM must equal or exceed the minimum required GM for that ship for the duration of the forthcoming voyage.
Principle	· a descriptive comprehensive and fundamental law, doctrine, or assumption, · a normative rule or code of conduct, or · a law or fact of nature underlying the working of an artificial device. The principle of any effect is the cause that produces it. Depending on the way the cause is understood the basic law governing that cause may acquire some distinction in its expression.

Chapter 2. FLUID STATICS

Chapter 2. FLUID STATICS

Rigid body
: In physics, a Rigid body is an idealization of a solid body of finite size in which deformation is neglected. In other words, the distance between any two given points of a Rigid body remains constant in time regardless of external forces exerted on it. Even though such an object cannot physically exist due to relativity, objects can normally be assumed to be perfectly rigid if they are not moving near the speed of light.

Fluid Pressure
: Fluid pressure is the pressure at some point within a fluid, such as water or air.
Fluid pressure occurs in one of two situations:

· an open condition, such as the ocean, a swimming pool, or the atmosphere; or
· a closed condition, such as a water line or a gas line.

Pressure in open conditions usually can be approximated as the pressure in "static" or non-moving conditions (even in the ocean where there are waves and currents), because the motions create only negligible changes in the pressure. Such conditions conform with principles of fluid statics.

Hydrometer
: A Hydrometer is an instrument used to measure the specific gravity (or relative density) of liquids; that is, the ratio of the density of the liquid to the density of water.
A Hydrometer is usually made of glass and consists of a cylindrical stem and a bulb weighted with mercury or lead shot to make it float upright. The liquid to be tested is poured into a tall jar, and the Hydrometer is gently lowered into the liquid until it floats freely.

Chapter 2. FLUID STATICS

Chapter 3. ELEMENTARY FLUID DYNAMICS-THE BERNOULLI EQUATION

Acceleration	Acceleration is the rate of change of velocity. At any point on a trajectory, the magnitude of the Acceleration is given by the rate of change of velocity in both magnitude and direction at that point. The true Acceleration at time t is found in the limit as time interval $\Delta t \to 0$. Components of Acceleration for a planar curved motion.
Fluid	A Fluid is a substance that continually deforms (flows) under an applied shear stress. All gases are Fluids, but not all liquids are Fluids. Fluids are a subset of the phases of matter and include liquids, gases, plasmas and, to some extent, plastic solids.
Energy	Nuclear potential Energy, along with electric potential Energy, provides the Energy released from nuclear fission and nuclear fusion processes. The result of both these processes are nuclei in which the more-optimal size of the nucleus allows the nuclear force (which is opposed by the electromagnetic force) to bind nuclear particles more tightly together than before the reaction. The Weak nuclear force provides the potential Energy for certain kinds of radioactive decay, such as beta decay.
Discharge pressure	Discharge pressure is the pressure generated on the output side of a gas compressor in a refrigeration or air conditioning system. The Discharge pressure is affected by several factors: size and speed of the condenser fan, condition and cleanliness of the condenser coil, and the size of the discharge line. An extremely high Discharge pressure coupled with an extremely low suction pressure is an indicator of a refrigerant restriction.
Kinetic energy	The kinetic Energy of an object is the extra energy which it possesses due to its motion. It is defined as the work needed to accelerate a body of a given mass from rest to its current velocity. Having gained this energy during its acceleration, the body maintains this kinetic Energy unless its speed changes.
Potential energy	Potential Energy is energy stored within a physical system as a result of the position or configuration of the different parts of that system. It is called potential Energy because it has the potential to be converted into other forms of energy, such as kinetic energy, and to do work in the process. The SI unit of measure for energy (including potential Energy) and work is the joule (symbol J).
Pressure head	Pressure head is a term used in fluid mechanics to represent the internal energy of a fluid due to the pressure exerted on its container. It may also be called static Pressure head or simply static head (but not static head pressure). It is mathematically expressed as: $$\psi = \frac{p}{\gamma} = \frac{p}{\rho g}$$ where ψ is Pressure head (Length, typically in units of m); p is fluid pressure (Force per unit Area, often as kPa units); and γ is the specific weight (Weight per unit volume, typically $N \cdot m^{-3}$ units) ρ is the density of the fluid (Mass per unit volume, typically $kg \cdot m^{-3}$)

Chapter 3. ELEMENTARY FLUID DYNAMICS-THE BERNOULLI EQUATION

Chapter 3. ELEMENTARY FLUID DYNAMICS-THE BERNOULLI EQUATION

g is acceleration due to gravity (rate of change of velocity, given in m·s^{-2})

A Venturi meter with two pressure instruments.

Velocity

In physics, velocity is the rate of change of position. It is a vector physical quantity; both speed and direction are required to define it. In the SI (metric) system, it is measured in meters per second: (m/s) or ms^{-1}.

Dynamic pressure

In incompressible fluid dynamics Dynamic pressure (indicated with q, or Q, and sometimes called velocity pressure or impact pressure) is the quantity defined by:

$$q = \tfrac{1}{2} \rho v^2,$$

where (using SI units):
Dynamic pressure is closely related to the kinetic energy of a fluid particle, since both quantities are proportional to the particle"s mass (through the density, in the case of Dynamic pressure) and square of the velocity. Dynamic pressure is in fact one of the terms of Bernoulli"s equation, which is essentially an equation of energy conservation for a fluid in motion. The Dynamic pressure is equal to the difference between the stagnation pressure and the static pressure.

Stagnation pressure

In fluid dynamics, Stagnation pressure is the static pressure at a stagnation point in a fluid flow. At a stagnation point the fluid velocity is zero and all kinetic energy has been converted into pressure energy. Stagnation pressure is equal to the sum of the free-stream dynamic pressure and free-stream static pressure.

Static

Statics is the branch of mechanics concerned with the analysis of loads (force, torque/moment) on physical systems in Static equilibrium, that is, in a state where the relative positions of subsystems do not vary over time, the system is either at rest, or its center of mass moves at constant velocity. The study of moving bodies is known as dynamics.

Static pressure

In fluid mechanics the term Static pressure has several uses:

· In the design and operation of aircraft, Static pressure is the air pressure in the aircraft"s Static pressure system.
· In fluid dynamics, Static pressure is the pressure at a nominated point in a fluid. Many authors use the term Static pressure in place of pressure to avoid ambiguity.
· The term Static pressure is also used by some authors in fluid statics.
An aircraft"s altimeter is operated by the Static pressure system.

Flow measurement

Flow measurement is the quantification of bulk fluid movement. It can be measured in a variety of ways. Both gas and liquid flow can be measured in volumetric or mass flow rates, such as litres per second or kilograms per second.

Chapter 3. ELEMENTARY FLUID DYNAMICS-THE BERNOULLI EQUATION

Chapter 3. ELEMENTARY FLUID DYNAMICS-THE BERNOULLI EQUATION

Pitot	A pitot tube is a pressure measurement instrument used to measure fluid flow velocity. The pitot tube was invented by the French engineer Henri pitot in the early 1700s and was modified to its modern form in the mid 1800s by French scientist Henry Darcy. It is widely used to determine the airspeed of an aircraft and to measure air and gas velocities in industrial applications.
Pitot-static	A pitot-static system is a system of pressure-sensitive instruments that is most often used in aviation to determine an aircraft"s airspeed, Mach number, altitude, and altitude trend. A pitot-static system generally consists of a pitot tube, a static port, and the pitot-static instruments. This equipment is used to measure the forces acting on a vehicle as a function of the temperature, density, pressure and viscosity of the fluid in which it is operating.
External flow	In fluid mechanics, external flow is such a flow that boundary layers develop freely, without constraints imposed by adjacent surfaces. Accordingly, there will always exist a region of the flow outside the boundary layer in which velocity, temperature, and/or concentration gradients are negligible.It can be defined as the flow of a fluid around a body that is completely submerged in it. An example includes fluid motion over a flat plate (inclined or parallel to the free stream velocity) and flow over curved surfaces such as a sphere, cylinder, airfoil, or turbine blade,air flowing around an airplane and water flowing around the submarines.
Vena contracta	Vena contracta is the point in a fluid stream where the diameter of the stream is the least, such as in the case of a stream issuing out of a nozzle, (orifice). (Evangelista Torricelli, 1643). The maximum contraction takes place at a section slightly on the downstream side of the orifice, where the jet is more or less horizontal.
Conservation of energy	The law of Conservation of energy is an empirical law of physics. It states that the total amount of energy in a closed system remains constant over time (are said to be conserved over time). A consequence of this law is that energy cannot be created nor destroyed.
Mass	In physics, Mass commonly refers to any of three properties of matter, which have been shown experimentally to be equivalent: inertial Mass, active gravitational Mass and passive gravitational Mass. In everyday usage, Mass is often taken to mean weight, but care should be taken to distinguish between the two terms in scientific use, as they actually refer to different properties. The inertial Mass of an object determines its acceleration in the presence of an applied force.
Volume	The density of an object is defined as mass per unit volume. The inverse of density is specific volume which is defined as volume divided by mass. volume and capacity are sometimes distinguished, with capacity being used for how much a container can hold (with contents measured commonly in liters or its derived units), and volume being how much space an object displaces (commonly measured in cubic meters or its derived units).

Chapter 3. ELEMENTARY FLUID DYNAMICS-THE BERNOULLI EQUATION

Chapter 3. ELEMENTARY FLUID DYNAMICS-THE BERNOULLI EQUATION

Compressible flow	Compressible fluid mechanics is a combination of the fields of traditional fluid mechanics and thermodynamics. It is related to the more general study of compressibility. In fluid dynamics, a flow is considered to be a Compressible flow if the density of the fluid changes with respect to pressure.
Control volume	In fluid mechanics and thermodynamics, a Control volume is a mathematical abstraction employed in the process of creating mathematical models of physical processes. In an inertial frame of reference, it is a fixed volume in space through which the fluid (gas or liquid) flows. The surface enclosing the Control volume is referred to as the control surface.
Cylinder	A cylinder is one of the most basic curvilinear geometric shapes, the surface formed by the points at a fixed distance from a given straight line, the axis of the cylinder. The solid enclosed by this surface and by two planes perpendicular to the axis is also called a cylinder. The surface area and the volume of a cylinder have been known since deep antiquity.
Incompressible flow	In fluid mechanics or more generally continuum mechanics, an Incompressible flow is solid or fluid flow in which the divergence of velocity is zero. This is more precisely termed isochoric flow. It is an idealization used to simplify analysis.
Cavitation	Cavitation is the formation of vapour bubbles of a flowing liquid in a region where the pressure of the liquid falls below its vapor pressure. Cavitation is usually divided into two classes of behavior: inertial (or transient) Cavitation, and noninertial Cavitation. Inertial Cavitation is the process where a void or bubble in a liquid rapidly collapses, producing a shock wave.
Nozzle	A Nozzle is a mechanical device designed to control the direction or characteristics of a fluid flow as it exits (or enters) an enclosed chamber or pipe via an orifice. A Nozzle is often a pipe or tube of varying cross sectional area, and it can be used to direct or modify the flow of a fluid (liquid or gas). Nozzles are frequently used to control the rate of flow, speed, direction, mass, shape, and/or the pressure of the stream that emerges from them.
Venturi effect	The Venturi effect is the reduction in fluid pressure that results when a fluid flows through a constricted section of pipe. The Venturi effect is named after Giovanni Battista Venturi, (1746-1822), an Italian physicist. The fluid velocity must increase through the constriction to satisfy the equation of continuity, while its pressure must decrease due to conservation of energy: the gain in kinetic energy is balanced by a drop in pressure or a pressure gradient force.
Internality	An internality is a term used in behavioral economics to describe those types of behaviors that impose costs on a person in the long-run that are not taken into account when making decisions in the present. Classical Economics discourages government from creating legislation that targets internalities, because it is assumed that the consumer takes these personal costs into account when paying for the good that causes the internality. For example, cigarettes should be taxed because of the negative consumption externalities that they impose, such as second-hand smoke, not because the smoker harms him or herself by smoking.

Chapter 3. ELEMENTARY FLUID DYNAMICS-THE BERNOULLI EQUATION

Chapter 3. ELEMENTARY FLUID DYNAMICS-THE BERNOULLI EQUATION

Hydraulic

The word "hydraulics" originates from the Greek word ὑδραυλικῆς which in turn originates from ὑδραυλος (hydraulos) meaning water organ which in turn comes from ὕδωρ and αὐλὅς. The earliest masters of hydraulics in the Greek-Hellenized West were Ctesibius (flourished c. 270 BC) and Hero of Alexandria (c. 10-80 AD). Hero describes a number of working machines using hydraulic power, such as the force pump, which is known from many Roman sites as having been used for raising water and in fire engines, for example.

Line

By defenition, a line is an infinite set of contiguous points in a plane that extend indefinitly in opposite directions such that the ratio of the verticle and horizontal displacements between any two points in the set is constant. In Euclidean geometry, a line is a straight curve. When geometry is used to model the real world, lines are used to represent straight objects with negligible width and height.

Hydraulic head

Hydraulic head or piezometric head is a specific measurement of water pressure above a geodetic datum. It is usually measured as a water surface elevation, expressed in units of length, at the entrance (or bottom) of a piezometer. In an aquifer, it can be calculated from the depth to water in a piezometric well (a specialized water well), and given information of the piezometer"s elevation and screen depth.

Pitot tube

A Pitot tube is a pressure measurement instrument used to measure fluid flow velocity. The Pitot tube was invented by the French engineer Henri Pitot in the early 1700s and was modified to its modern form in the mid 1800s by French scientist Henry Darcy. It is widely used to determine the airspeed of an aircraft and to measure air and gas velocities in industrial applications.

Compressibility

Compressibility is used in the Earth sciences to quantify the ability of a soil or rock to reduce in volume with applied pressure. This concept is important for specific storage, when estimating groundwater reserves in confined aquifers. Geologic materials are made up of two portions: solids and voids (or same as porosity).

Chapter 3. ELEMENTARY FLUID DYNAMICS-THE BERNOULLI EQUATION

Chapter 4. FLUID KINEMATICS

Fluid	A Fluid is a substance that continually deforms (flows) under an applied shear stress. All gases are Fluids, but not all liquids are Fluids. Fluids are a subset of the phases of matter and include liquids, gases, plasmas and, to some extent, plastic solids.
Kinematics	Kinematics is the branch of classical mechanics that describes the motion of objects without consideration of the causes leading to the motion. Kinematics is not to be confused with another branch of classical mechanics: analytical dynamics, sometimes subdivided into kinetics (the study of the relation between external forces and motion) and statics (the study of the relations in a system at equilibrium). Kinematics also differs from dynamics as used in modern-day physics to describe time-evolution of a system.
Velocity	In physics, velocity is the rate of change of position. It is a vector physical quantity; both speed and direction are required to define it. In the SI (metric) system, it is measured in meters per second: (m/s) or ms^{-1}.
Vector	In elementary mathematics, physics, and engineering, a vector is a geometric object that has both a magnitude (or length) and direction. A vector is frequently represented by a line segment with a definite direction, or graphically as an arrow, connecting an initial point A with a terminal point B, and denoted by $\overrightarrow{AB}$. A vector is what is needed to "carry" the point A to the point B; the Latin word vector means "one who carries". The magnitude of the vector is the distance between the two points and the direction refers to the direction of displacement from A to B. Many algebraic operations on real numbers such as addition, subtraction, multiplication, and negation have close analogues fs, operations which obey the familiar algebraic laws of commutativity, associativity, and distributivity.
Lagrangian	The Lagrangian, L, of a dynamical system is a function that summarizes the dynamics of the system. It is named after Joseph Louis Lagrange. The concept of a Lagrangian was originally introduced in a reformulation of classical mechanics known as Lagrangian mechanics.
Acceleration	Acceleration is the rate of change of velocity. At any point on a trajectory, the magnitude of the Acceleration is given by the rate of change of velocity in both magnitude and direction at that point. The true Acceleration at time t is found in the limit as time interval Δt → 0. Components of Acceleration for a planar curved motion.
Material derivative	The Material derivative is a derivative taken along a path moving with velocity v, and is often used in fluid mechanics and classical mechanics. It describes the time rate of change of some quantity (such as heat or momentum) by following it, while moving with a - space and time dependent - velocity field. For example, in fluid dynamics, take the case that the velocity field under consideration is the flow velocity itself, and the quantity of interest is the temperature of the fluid.

Chapter 4. FLUID KINEMATICS

Chapter 4. FLUID KINEMATICS

Particle Acceleration | In a compressible sound transmission medium - mainly air - air particles get an accelerated motion: the particle acceleration or sound acceleration with the symbol a in metre/second^2. In acoustics or physics, acceleration (symbol: a) is defined as the rate of change (or time derivative) of velocity. It is thus a vector quantity with dimension length/time^2.

Control volume | In fluid mechanics and thermodynamics, a Control volume is a mathematical abstraction employed in the process of creating mathematical models of physical processes. In an inertial frame of reference, it is a fixed volume in space through which the fluid (gas or liquid) flows. The surface enclosing the Control volume is referred to as the control surface.

Extensive property | In the physical sciences, an intensive property, is a physical property of a system that does not depend on the system size or the amount of material in the system: it is scale invariant. By contrast, an Extensive property of a system does depend on the system size or the amount of material in the system. Some intensive properties, such as viscosity, are empirical macroscopic quantities and are not relevant to extremely small systems.

Intensive property | In the physical sciences, an Intensive property, is a physical property of a system that does not depend on the system size or the amount of material in the system: it is scale invariant. By contrast, an extensive property of a system does depend on the system size or the amount of material in the system. Some intensive properties, such as viscosity, are empirical macroscopic quantities and are not relevant to extremely small systems.

Chapter 4. FLUID KINEMATICS

Chapter 5. FINITE CONTROL VOLUME ANALYSIS

Conservation of energy	The law of Conservation of energy is an empirical law of physics. It states that the total amount of energy in a closed system remains constant over time (are said to be conserved over time). A consequence of this law is that energy cannot be created nor destroyed.
Control volume	In fluid mechanics and thermodynamics, a Control volume is a mathematical abstraction employed in the process of creating mathematical models of physical processes. In an inertial frame of reference, it is a fixed volume in space through which the fluid (gas or liquid) flows. The surface enclosing the Control volume is referred to as the control surface.
Cylinder	A cylinder is one of the most basic curvilinear geometric shapes, the surface formed by the points at a fixed distance from a given straight line, the axis of the cylinder. The solid enclosed by this surface and by two planes perpendicular to the axis is also called a cylinder. The surface area and the volume of a cylinder have been known since deep antiquity.
Mass	In physics, Mass commonly refers to any of three properties of matter, which have been shown experimentally to be equivalent: inertial Mass, active gravitational Mass and passive gravitational Mass. In everyday usage, Mass is often taken to mean weight, but care should be taken to distinguish between the two terms in scientific use, as they actually refer to different properties. The inertial Mass of an object determines its acceleration in the presence of an applied force.
Velocity	In physics, velocity is the rate of change of position. It is a vector physical quantity; both speed and direction are required to define it. In the SI (metric) system, it is measured in meters per second: (m/s) or ms^{-1}.
Incompressible flow	In fluid mechanics or more generally continuum mechanics, an Incompressible flow is solid or fluid flow in which the divergence of velocity is zero. This is more precisely termed isochoric flow. It is an idealization used to simplify analysis.
Maxima	In mathematics, maxima and minima, known collectively as extrema (singular: extremum), are the largest value (maximum) or smallest value (minimum), that a function takes in a point either within a given neighbourhood (local extremum) or on the function domain in its entirety (global extremum). More generally, the maxima and minima of a set (as defined in in set theory) are the greatest and least values in the set. A real-valued function f defined on a real line is said to have a local (or relative) maximum point at the point x^*, if there exists some $\varepsilon > 0$ such that $f(x^*) \geq f(x)$ when $|x - x^*| < \varepsilon$.
Relative velocity	In kinematics, Relative velocity is the vector difference between the velocities of two objects, as evaluated in terms of a single coordinate system, usually an inertial frame of reference unless specifically stated otherwise. For example, if the velocities of particles A and B are $\mathbf{V}_A$ and $\mathbf{V}_B$ respectively in terms of a given inertial coordinate system, then the Relative velocity of A with respect to B (also called the velocity of A relative to B, or $\mathbf{V}_{A\ rel\ B}$) is $\mathbf{V}_{A\ rel\ B} = \mathbf{V}_A - \mathbf{V}_B.$ Conversely, the velocity of B relative to A is

Chapter 5. FINITE CONTROL VOLUME ANALYSIS

Chapter 5. FINITE CONTROL VOLUME ANALYSIS

$$\mathbf{V}_{B \text{ rel } A} = \mathbf{V}_B - \mathbf{V}_A.$$

Volume	The density of an object is defined as mass per unit volume. The inverse of density is specific volume which is defined as volume divided by mass. volume and capacity are sometimes distinguished, with capacity being used for how much a container can hold (with contents measured commonly in liters or its derived units), and volume being how much space an object displaces (commonly measured in cubic meters or its derived units).
Linear momentum	In classical mechanics, momentum is the product of the mass and velocity of an object . For more accurate measures of momentum, see the section "modern definitions of momentum" on this page. It is sometimes referred to as linear momentum to distinguish it from the related subject of angular momentum.
Momentum	In classical mechanics, Momentum is the product of the mass and velocity of an object . For more accurate measures of Momentum, see the section "modern definitions of Momentum" on this page. It is sometimes referred to as linear Momentum to distinguish it from the related subject of angular Momentum.
Flux	" In the various subfields of physics, there exist two common usages of the term Flux, both with rigorous mathematical frameworks. · In the study of transport phenomena (heat transfer, mass transfer and fluid dynamics), Flux is defined as the amount that flows through a unit area per unit time Flux in this definition is a vector. · In the field of electromagnetism and mathematics, Flux is usually the integral of a vector quantity over a finite surface. It is an integral operator and acts on a vector field as do the gradient, divergence and curl found in vector analysis. The result of this integration is a scalar quantity.
Body force	A Body force is a force that acts throughout the volume of a body. This is in contrast to surface forces, such as shear forces and normal forces, which are exerted only on the surface of the object. Gravity and electromagnetic forces are examples of Body forces.
Force	In physics, a Force has the capacity to change the motion of a free body or cause stress in a fixed body. It can also be described by intuitive concepts such as a push or pull that can cause an object with mass to change its velocity , i.e., to accelerate, or which can cause a flexible object to deform. Force has both magnitude and direction, making it a vector quantity.
Weber number	The Weber number is a dimensionless number in fluid mechanics that is often useful in analysing fluid flows where there is an interface between two different fluids, especially for multiphase flows with strongly curved surfaces. It can be thought of as a measure of the relative importance of the fluid"s inertia compared to its surface tension. The quantity is useful in analyzing thin film flows and the formation of droplets and bubbles. It is named after Moritz Weber (1871-1951) and may be written as:

Chapter 5. FINITE CONTROL VOLUME ANALYSIS

Chapter 5. FINITE CONTROL VOLUME ANALYSIS

$$We = \frac{\rho v^2 l}{\sigma}$$

where

- ρ is the density of the fluid.
- v is its velocity.
- l is its characteristic length, typically the droplet diameter.
- σ is the surface tension.

Torque

Torque,), is the tendency of a force to rotate an object about an axis, fulcrum, or pivot. Just as a force is a push or a pull, a Torque can be thought of as a twist.
In more basic terms, Torque measures how hard something is rotated.

Angular momentum

Angular momentum is a quantity that is useful in describing the rotational state of a physical system. For a rigid body rotating around an axis of symmetry (e.g. the fins of a ceiling fan), the Angular momentum can be expressed as the product of the body"s moment of inertia (A measure of an object"s resistance to changes in its rotation rate) and its angular velocity ($\mathbf{L} = I\boldsymbol{\omega}$). In this way, Angular momentum is sometimes described as the rotational analog of linear momentum.

Deformation

In continuum mechanics, Deformation is the change in shape and/or size of a continuum body after it undergoes a displacement between an initial or undeformed configuration $\kappa_0(\mathcal{B})$, at time $t = 0$, and a current or deformed configuration $\kappa_t(\mathcal{B})$, at the current time t.
In general, the displacement of a continuum body has two components: a rigid-body displacement component and a Deformation component. If after a displacement of the continuum there is a relative displacement between particles, a Deformation has occurred.

Power

In physics, power is the rate at which work is performed or energy is converted. It is an energy per unit of time. As a rate of change of work done or the energy of a subsystem, power is

$$P = \frac{W}{t}$$

where P is power, W is work and t is time.

Rule

A Rule is:

- Rewrite Rule, in generative grammar and computer science
- Standardization, a formal and widely-accepted statement, fact, definition, or qualification
- Operation, a determinate Rule (method) for performing a mathematical operation and obtaining a certain result (Mathematics, Logic)

Chapter 5. FINITE CONTROL VOLUME ANALYSIS

Chapter 5. FINITE CONTROL VOLUME ANALYSIS

· Unary operation
· Binary operation
· Rule of inference, a function from sets of formulae to formulae (Mathematics, Logic)
· Rule of thumb, principle with broad application that is not intended to be strictly accurate or reliable for every situation. Also often simply referred to as a Rule
· Moral, an atomic element of a moral code for guiding choices in human behavior
· Heuristic, a quantized "Rule" which shows a tendency or probability for successful function
· A regulation, as in sports
· A Production Rule, as in computer science
· Procedural law, a Ruleset governing the application of laws to cases

· A law, which may informally be called a "Rule"
· A court ruling, a decision by a court
· In the U.S. Government, a regulation mandated by Congress, but written or expanded upon by the Executive Branch.
· Norm (sociology), an informal but widely accepted Rule, concept, truth, definition, or qualification (social norms, legal norms, coding norms)
· Norm (philosophy), a kind of sentence or a reason to act, feel or believe
· Governance:

· Military Rule, governance by a military body
· Monastic Rule, a collection of precepts that guides the life of monks or nuns in a religious order where the superior holds the place of Christ
· Slide Rule

· "Rule," a song by Ayumi Hamasaki
· "Rule," a song by rapper Nas
· "Rules," an album by the band The Whitest Boy Alive
· Rules: Pyaar Ka Superhit Formula, a 2003 Bollywood film
· Ruler, an instrument for measuring lengths
· Rule, a component of an astrolabe, circumferator or similar instrument
· The Rules, a bestselling self-help book
· Rule Project (Run Up-to-date Linux Everywhere), a project that aims to use up-to-date Linux software on old PCs
· Rule engine, a software system that helps managing business Rules
· Ja Rule, a hip hop artist

· R.U.L.E., a 2005 greatest hits album by rapper Ja Rule
· "Rules," a KMFDM song "

Fluid | A Fluid is a substance that continually deforms (flows) under an applied shear stress. All gases are Fluids, but not all liquids are Fluids. Fluids are a subset of the phases of matter and include liquids, gases, plasmas and, to some extent, plastic solids.

Chapter 5. FINITE CONTROL VOLUME ANALYSIS

Chapter 5. FINITE CONTROL VOLUME ANALYSIS

Machine	A machine is any device that uses energy to perform some activity. In common usage, the meaning is that of a device having parts that perform or assist in performing any type of work. A simple machine is a device that transforms the direction or magnitude of a force without consuming any energy.
Energy	Nuclear potential Energy, along with electric potential Energy, provides the Energy released from nuclear fission and nuclear fusion processes. The result of both these processes are nuclei in which the more-optimal size of the nucleus allows the nuclear force (which is opposed by the electromagnetic force) to bind nuclear particles more tightly together than before the reaction. The Weak nuclear force provides the potential Energy for certain kinds of radioactive decay, such as beta decay.
Heat transfer	Heat transfer is the transition of thermal energy from a hotter object to a cooler object ("object" in this sense designating a complex collection of particles which is capable of storing energy in many different ways). When an object or fluid is at a different temperature than its surroundings or another object, transfer of thermal energy, also known as heat transfer, or heat exchange, occurs in such a way that the body and the surroundings reach thermal equilibrium, this means that they are at the same temprature. heat transfer always occurs from a higher-temperature object to a cooler temperature one as described by the second law of thermodynamics or the Clausius statement.
Internality	An internality is a term used in behavioral economics to describe those types of behaviors that impose costs on a person in the long-run that are not taken into account when making decisions in the present. Classical Economics discourages government from creating legislation that targets internalities, because it is assumed that the consumer takes these personal costs into account when paying for the good that causes the internality. For example, cigarettes should be taxed because of the negative consumption externalities that they impose, such as second-hand smoke, not because the smoker harms him or herself by smoking.
Internal energy	In thermodynamics, the Internal energy of a thermodynamic system, denoted by U, or , is the total of the kinetic energy due to the motion of particles (translational, rotational, vibrational) and the potential energy associated with the vibrational and electric energy of atoms within molecules or crystals. It includes the energy in all of the chemical bonds, and the energy of the free, conduction electrons in metals. One can also calculate the Internal energy of electromagnetic or black body radiation.
Kinetic energy	The kinetic Energy of an object is the extra energy which it possesses due to its motion. It is defined as the work needed to accelerate a body of a given mass from rest to its current velocity. Having gained this energy during its acceleration, the body maintains this kinetic Energy unless its speed changes.
Thermodynamics	Other Related Topics · Engineering Thermodynamics · Entropy for Beginners

Chapter 5. FINITE CONTROL VOLUME ANALYSIS

Chapter 5. FINITE CONTROL VOLUME ANALYSIS

Newtonian fluid

A Newtonian fluid is a fluid whose stress versus strain rate curve is linear and passes through the origin. The constant of proportionality is known as the viscosity.

A simple equation to describe Newtonian fluid behaviour is

$$\tau = \mu \frac{du}{dy}$$

where

τ is the shear stress exerted by the fluid ("drag") [Pa]

μ is the fluid viscosity - a constant of proportionality [Pa·s]

$\frac{du}{dy}$ is the velocity gradient perpendicular to the direction of shear [s^{-1}]

In common terms, this means the fluid continues to flow, regardless of the forces acting on it.

Stress

In linguistics, stress is the relative emphasis that may be given to certain syllables in a word. The term is also used for similar patterns of phonetic prominence inside syllables. The word accent is sometimes also used with this sense.

Sign convention

In physics, a sign convention is a choice of the signs (plus or minus) of a set of quantities, in a case where the choice of sign is arbitrary. "Arbitrary" here means that the same physical system can be correctly described using different choices for the signs, as long as one set of definitions is used consistently. The choices made may differ between authors.

Shear stress

A Shear stress, $\mathcal{T}$ is applied to the top of the square while the bottom is held in place. This stress results in a strain, or deformation, changing the square into a parallelogram.

A Shear stress, denoted $\mathcal{T}$ (tau), is defined as a stress which is applied parallel or tangential to a face of a material, as opposed to a normal stress which is applied perpendicularly.

The formula to calculate average Shear stress is:

$$\tau = \frac{F}{A}$$

where

τ = the Shear stress

F = the force applied

A = the cross sectional area

Beam shear is defined as the internal Shear stress of a beam caused by the shear force applied to the beam.

Shearing

Shearing in continuum mechanics refers to the occurrence of a shear strain, which is a deformation of a material substance in which parallel internal surfaces slide past one another. It is induced by a shear stress in the material. Shear strain is distinguished from volumetric strain, the change in a material"s volume in response to stress.

Chapter 5. FINITE CONTROL VOLUME ANALYSIS

Chapter 5. FINITE CONTROL VOLUME ANALYSIS

Enthalpy	In thermodynamics and molecular chemistry, Enthalpy (denoted as H) is a thermodynamic property of a thermodynamic system. It can be used to calculate the heat transfer during a quasistatic process taking place in a closed thermodynamic system under constant pressure (isobaric process). Change in Enthalpy ΔH is frequently a more useful value than H - for quasistatic processes that occur under constant pressure conditions, ΔH is equal to the change in the internal energy of the system, plus the work that the system has done on its surroundings.
Hydraulic head	Hydraulic head or piezometric head is a specific measurement of water pressure above a geodetic datum. It is usually measured as a water surface elevation, expressed in units of length, at the entrance (or bottom) of a piezometer. In an aquifer, it can be calculated from the depth to water in a piezometric well (a specialized water well), and given information of the piezometer"s elevation and screen depth.
Flow measurement	Flow measurement is the quantification of bulk fluid movement. It can be measured in a variety of ways. Both gas and liquid flow can be measured in volumetric or mass flow rates, such as litres per second or kilograms per second.
Discharge pressure	Discharge pressure is the pressure generated on the output side of a gas compressor in a refrigeration or air conditioning system. The Discharge pressure is affected by several factors: size and speed of the condenser fan, condition and cleanliness of the condenser coil, and the size of the discharge line. An extremely high Discharge pressure coupled with an extremely low suction pressure is an indicator of a refrigerant restriction.
Mechanical energy	In physics, Mechanical energy describes the sum of potential energy and kinetic energy present in the components of a mechanical system. Scientists make simplifying assumptions to make calculations about how mechanical systems react. For example, instead of calculating the Mechanical energy separately for each of the billions of molecules in a soccer ball, it is easier to treat the entire ball as one object.
Potential energy	Potential Energy is energy stored within a physical system as a result of the position or configuration of the different parts of that system. It is called potential Energy because it has the potential to be converted into other forms of energy, such as kinetic energy, and to do work in the process. The SI unit of measure for energy (including potential Energy) and work is the joule (symbol J).
Pressure head	Pressure head is a term used in fluid mechanics to represent the internal energy of a fluid due to the pressure exerted on its container. It may also be called static Pressure head or simply static head (but not static head pressure). It is mathematically expressed as: $$\psi = \frac{p}{\gamma} = \frac{p}{\rho g}$$ where ψ is Pressure head (Length, typically in units of m); p is fluid pressure (Force per unit Area, often as kPa units); and γ is the specific weight (Weight per unit volume, typically N·m^{-3} units)

Chapter 5. FINITE CONTROL VOLUME ANALYSIS

Chapter 5. FINITE CONTROL VOLUME ANALYSIS

ρ is the density of the fluid (Mass per unit volume, typically kg·m⁻³)
g is acceleration due to gravity (rate of change of velocity, given in m·s⁻²)

A Venturi meter with two pressure instruments.

Chapter 5. FINITE CONTROL VOLUME ANALYSIS

Chapter 6. DIFFERENTIAL ANALYSIS OF FLUID FLOW

Acceleration	Acceleration is the rate of change of velocity. At any point on a trajectory, the magnitude of the Acceleration is given by the rate of change of velocity in both magnitude and direction at that point. The true Acceleration at time t is found in the limit as time interval Δt → 0. Components of Acceleration for a planar curved motion.
Control volume	In fluid mechanics and thermodynamics, a Control volume is a mathematical abstraction employed in the process of creating mathematical models of physical processes. In an inertial frame of reference, it is a fixed volume in space through which the fluid (gas or liquid) flows. The surface enclosing the Control volume is referred to as the control surface.
Fluid	A Fluid is a substance that continually deforms (flows) under an applied shear stress. All gases are Fluids, but not all liquids are Fluids. Fluids are a subset of the phases of matter and include liquids, gases, plasmas and, to some extent, plastic solids.
Kinematics	Kinematics is the branch of classical mechanics that describes the motion of objects without consideration of the causes leading to the motion. Kinematics is not to be confused with another branch of classical mechanics: analytical dynamics, sometimes subdivided into kinetics (the study of the relation between external forces and motion) and statics (the study of the relations in a system at equilibrium). Kinematics also differs from dynamics as used in modern-day physics to describe time-evolution of a system.
Velocity	In physics, velocity is the rate of change of position. It is a vector physical quantity; both speed and direction are required to define it. In the SI (metric) system, it is measured in meters per second: (m/s) or ms^{-1}.
Deformation	In continuum mechanics, Deformation is the change in shape and/or size of a continuum body after it undergoes a displacement between an initial or undeformed configuration $\kappa_0(\mathcal{B})$, at time $t=0$, and a current or deformed configuration $\kappa_t(\mathcal{B})$, at the current time t. In general, the displacement of a continuum body has two components: a rigid-body displacement component and a Deformation component. If after a displacement of the continuum there is a relative displacement between particles, a Deformation has occurred.
Material derivative	The Material derivative is a derivative taken along a path moving with velocity v, and is often used in fluid mechanics and classical mechanics. It describes the time rate of change of some quantity (such as heat or momentum) by following it, while moving with a - space and time dependent - velocity field. For example, in fluid dynamics, take the case that the velocity field under consideration is the flow velocity itself, and the quantity of interest is the temperature of the fluid.
Rotation	A Rotation is a movement of an object in a circular motion. A two-dimensional object rotates around a center (or point) of Rotation. A three-dimensional object rotates around a line called an axis.

Chapter 6. DIFFERENTIAL ANALYSIS OF FLUID FLOW

Chapter 6. DIFFERENTIAL ANALYSIS OF FLUID FLOW

Vector	In elementary mathematics, physics, and engineering, a vector is a geometric object that has both a magnitude (or length) and direction. A vector is frequently represented by a line segment with a definite direction, or graphically as an arrow, connecting an initial point A with a terminal point B, and denoted by $\overrightarrow{AB}$. A vector is what is needed to "carry" the point A to the point B; the Latin word vector means "one who carries". The magnitude of the vector is the distance between the two points and the direction refers to the direction of displacement from A to B. Many algebraic operations on real numbers such as addition, subtraction, multiplication, and negation have close analogues fs, operations which obey the familiar algebraic laws of commutativity, associativity, and distributivity.
Shearing	Shearing in continuum mechanics refers to the occurrence of a shear strain, which is a deformation of a material substance in which parallel internal surfaces slide past one another. It is induced by a shear stress in the material. Shear strain is distinguished from volumetric strain, the change in a material"s volume in response to stress.
Strain rate	Strain rate, with regards to materials science, is the change in strain over the change in time and is denoted as $\hat{\imath}$. $\hat{\imath} = \delta\varepsilon/\delta t$ Strain rate is rate of deformation We have $$\hat{\imath} = \delta\varepsilon/\delta t = \frac{1}{\ell_0}\frac{d\ell}{dt} = \frac{v}{\ell_0}$$ where ℓ_0 is the original length and v is the speed of deformation. In a Newtonian fluid, the relation between the shear stress and the rate of strain is linear, the constant of proportionality being the coefficient of viscosity.
Conservation of energy	The law of Conservation of energy is an empirical law of physics. It states that the total amount of energy in a closed system remains constant over time (are said to be conserved over time). A consequence of this law is that energy cannot be created nor destroyed.
Mass	In physics, Mass commonly refers to any of three properties of matter, which have been shown experimentally to be equivalent: inertial Mass, active gravitational Mass and passive gravitational Mass. In everyday usage, Mass is often taken to mean weight, but care should be taken to distinguish between the two terms in scientific use, as they actually refer to different properties. The inertial Mass of an object determines its acceleration in the presence of an applied force.
Cylinder	A cylinder is one of the most basic curvilinear geometric shapes, the surface formed by the points at a fixed distance from a given straight line, the axis of the cylinder. The solid enclosed by this surface and by two planes perpendicular to the axis is also called a cylinder. The surface area and the volume of a cylinder have been known since deep antiquity.

Chapter 6. DIFFERENTIAL ANALYSIS OF FLUID FLOW

Chapter 6. DIFFERENTIAL ANALYSIS OF FLUID FLOW

Cartesian coordinate system

A Cartesian coordinate system specifies each point uniquely in a plane by a pair of numerical coordinates, which are the signed distances from the point to two fixed perpendicular directed lines, measured in the same unit of length.

Each reference line is called a coordinate axis or just axis of the system, and the point where they meet is its origin. The coordinates can also be defined as the positions of the perpendicular projections of the point onto the two axes, expressed as a signed distances from the origin.

Incompressible flow

In fluid mechanics or more generally continuum mechanics, an Incompressible flow is solid or fluid flow in which the divergence of velocity is zero. This is more precisely termed isochoric flow. It is an idealization used to simplify analysis.

Polar coordinate

In mathematics, the polar coordinate system is a two-dimensional coordinate system in which each point on a plane is determined by a distance from a fixed point and an angle from a fixed direction.

The fixed point (analogous to the origin of a Cartesian system) is called the pole, and the ray from the pole with the fixed direction is the polar axis. The distance from the pole is called the radial coordinate or radius, and the angle is the angular coordinate, polar angle, or azimuth.

Stream function

One way is to define the Stream function ψ for a two dimensional flow such that the flow velocity can be expressed as:
$$\mathbf{u} = \nabla \times \boldsymbol{\psi}$$
Where $\boldsymbol{\psi} = (0, 0, \psi)$ if the velocity vector $\mathbf{u} = (u, v, 0)$.
In Cartesian coordinate system this is equivalent to
$$u = \frac{\partial \psi}{\partial y}, \qquad v = -\frac{\partial \psi}{\partial x}$$
Where u and v are the velocities in the x and y coordinate directions, respectively.
Another definition (used more widely in meteorology and oceanography than the above) is
$$\mathbf{u} = \mathbf{z} \times \nabla \psi' \equiv (-\psi'_y, \psi'_x, 0)$$
where $\mathbf{z}$ is a unit vector in the + z direction and the subscripts indicate partial derivatives.

Momentum

In classical mechanics, Momentum is the product of the mass and velocity of an object. For more accurate measures of Momentum, see the section "modern definitions of Momentum" on this page. It is sometimes referred to as linear Momentum to distinguish it from the related subject of angular Momentum.

Body force

A Body force is a force that acts throughout the volume of a body. This is in contrast to surface forces, such as shear forces and normal forces, which are exerted only on the surface of the object. Gravity and electromagnetic forces are examples of Body forces.

Chapter 6. DIFFERENTIAL ANALYSIS OF FLUID FLOW

Chapter 6. DIFFERENTIAL ANALYSIS OF FLUID FLOW

Force	In physics, a Force has the capacity to change the motion of a free body or cause stress in a fixed body. It can also be described by intuitive concepts such as a push or pull that can cause an object with mass to change its velocity , i.e., to accelerate, or which can cause a flexible object to deform. Force has both magnitude and direction, making it a vector quantity.
Newtonian fluid	A Newtonian fluid is a fluid whose stress versus strain rate curve is linear and passes through the origin. The constant of proportionality is known as the viscosity. A simple equation to describe Newtonian fluid behaviour is $$\tau = \mu \frac{du}{dy}$$ where τ is the shear stress exerted by the fluid ("drag") [Pa] μ is the fluid viscosity - a constant of proportionality [PaÂ·s] $\frac{du}{dy}$ is the velocity gradient perpendicular to the direction of shear [s^{-1}] In common terms, this means the fluid continues to flow, regardless of the forces acting on it.
Stress	In linguistics, stress is the relative emphasis that may be given to certain syllables in a word. The term is also used for similar patterns of phonetic prominence inside syllables. The word accent is sometimes also used with this sense.
Stress field	A Stress field is a region in a body for which the stress is defined at every point. Stress fields are widely used in fluid dynamics and materials science. Intuitively, one can picture the Stress fields as the stress created by adding an extra half plane of atoms to a crystal.
Sign convention	In physics, a sign convention is a choice of the signs (plus or minus) of a set of quantities, in a case where the choice of sign is arbitrary. "Arbitrary" here means that the same physical system can be correctly described using different choices for the signs, as long as one set of definitions is used consistently. The choices made may differ between authors.
Potential flow	In fluid dynamics, potential flow describes the velocity field as the gradient of a scalar function: the velocity potential. As a result, a potential flow is characterized by an irrotational velocity field, which is a valid approximation for several applications. The irrotationality of a potential flow is due to the curl of a gradient always being equal to zero.
Flow network	In graph theory, a flow network is a directed graph where each edge has a capacity and each edge receives a flow. The amount of flow on an edge cannot exceed the capacity of the edge. Often in Operations Research, a directed graph is called a network, the vertices are called nodes and the edges are called arcs.

Chapter 6. DIFFERENTIAL ANALYSIS OF FLUID FLOW

Chapter 6. DIFFERENTIAL ANALYSIS OF FLUID FLOW

Line	By defenition, a line is an infinite set of contiguous points in a plane that extend indefinitely in opposite directions such that the ratio of the verticle and horizontal displacements between any two points in the set is constant. In Euclidean geometry, a line is a straight curve. When geometry is used to model the real world, lines are used to represent straight objects with negligible width and height.
Strength	In materials science, the strength of a material is its ability to withstand an applied stress without failure. Yield strength refers to the point on the engineering stress-strain curve (as opposed to true stress-strain curve) beyond which the material begins deformation that cannot be reversed upon removal of the loading. Ultimate strength refers to the point on the engineering stress-strain curve corresponding to the maximum stress.
No-slip condition	In fluid dynamics, the No-slip condition for viscous fluid states that at a solid boundary, the fluid will have zero velocity relative to the boundary. The fluid velocity at all fluid-solid boundaries is equal to that of the solid boundary. Conceptually, one can think of the outermost molecules of fluid as stuck to the surfaces past which it flows.
Drag coefficient	In fluid dynamics, the drag coefficient (commonly denoted as C_d, C_x or C_w) is a dimensionless quantity that is used to quantify the drag or resistance of an object in a fluid environment such as air or water. It is used in the drag equation, where a lower drag coefficient indicates the object will have less aerodynamic or hydrodynamic drag. The drag coefficient is always associated with a particular surface area.
Pressure coefficient	The pressure coefficient is a dimensionless number which describes the relative pressures throughout a flow field in fluid dynamics. The pressure coefficient is used in aerodynamics and hydrodynamics. Every point in a fluid flow field has its own unique pressure coefficient, C_p.
Airfoil	An Airfoil or aerofoil is the shape of a wing or blade (of a propeller, rotor or turbine) or sail as seen in cross-section. An Airfoil-shaped body moved through a fluid produces a force perpendicular to the motion called lift. Subsonic flight Airfoils have a characteristic shape with a rounded leading edge, followed by a sharp trailing edge, often with asymmetric camber.
Drag Force	In fluid dynamics, drag refers to forces that oppose the relative motion of an object through a fluid (a liquid or gas). Drag forces act in a direction opposite to the oncoming flow velocity. Unlike other resistive forces such as dry friction, which is nearly independent of velocity, Drag forces depend on velocity.
Lift	A fluid flowing past the surface of a body exerts a force on it. Lift is defined to be the component of this force that is perpendicular to the oncoming flow direction. It contrasts with the drag force, which is defined to be the component of the fluid-dynamic force parallel to the flow direction.
Lift coefficient	The Lift coefficient (C_L or C_Z) is a dimensionless coefficient that relates the lift generated by an airfoil, the dynamic pressure of the fluid flow around the airfoil, and the planform area of the airfoil. It may also be described as the ratio of lift pressure to dynamic pressure.

Chapter 6. DIFFERENTIAL ANALYSIS OF FLUID FLOW

Chapter 6. DIFFERENTIAL ANALYSIS OF FLUID FLOW

Lift coefficient may be used to relate the total lift generated by an aircraft to the total area of the wing of the aircraft. In this application it is called the aircraft Lift coefficient C_L.

The Lift coefficient C_L is equal to:

$$C_L = \frac{L}{\frac{1}{2}\rho v^2 A} = \frac{L}{qA}$$

where

- L is the lift force,
- ρ is fluid density,
- v is true airspeed,
- q is dynamic pressure, and
- A is planform area.

Navier-Stokes equations

The Navier-Stokes equations describe the motion of fluid substances, that is substances which can flow. These equations arise from applying Newton"s second law to fluid motion, together with the assumption that the fluid stress is the sum of a diffusing viscous term (proportional to the gradient of velocity), plus a pressure term.

They are exceptionally useful because they describe the physics of many things of academic and economic interest.

Boundary layer

In physics and fluid mechanics, a Boundary layer is that layer of fluid in the immediate vicinity of a bounding surface. In the Earth"s atmosphere, the planetary Boundary layer is the air layer near the ground affected by diurnal heat, moisture or momentum transfer to or from the surface. On an aircraft wing the Boundary layer is the part of the flow close to the wing.

Couette flow

In fluid dynamics, Couette flow refers to the laminar flow of a viscous fluid in the space between two parallel plates, one of which is moving relative to the other. The flow is driven by virtue of viscous drag force acting on the fluid and the applied pressure gradient parallel to the plates. This type of flow is named in honor of Maurice Marie Alfred Couette, a Professor of Physics at the French university of Angers in the late 19th century.

Computational fluid dynamics

Computational fluid dynamics is one of the branches of fluid mechanics that uses numerical methods and algorithms to solve and analyze problems that involve fluid flows. Computers are used to perform the millions of calculations required to simulate the interaction of liquids and gases with surfaces defined by boundary conditions. Even with high-speed supercomputers only approximate solutions can be achieved in many cases.

Chapter 6. DIFFERENTIAL ANALYSIS OF FLUID FLOW

Chapter 7. SIMILITUDE, DIMENSIONAL ANALYSIS, AND MODELING

Dimensional analysis

In mathematics and science, Dimensional analysis is a tool to understand the properties of physical quantities independent of the units used to measure them. Every physical quantity is some combination of mass, length, time, electric charge, and temperature, (denoted M, L, T, Q, and Θ, respectively). For example, velocity, which may be measured in meters per second (m/s), miles per hour (mi/h), or some other units, has dimension L/T.

Dimensional analysis is routinely used to check the plausibility of derived equations and computations.

Euler numbers

In the area of number theory, the Euler numbers are a sequence E_n of integers defined by the following Taylor series expansion:

$$\frac{1}{\cosh t} = \frac{2}{e^t + e^{-t}} = \sum_{n=0}^{\infty} \frac{E_n}{n!} \cdot t^n$$

where cosh t is the hyperbolic cosine. The Euler numbers appear as a special value of the Euler polynomials.

The odd-indexed Euler numbers are all zero.

Force

In physics, a Force has the capacity to change the motion of a free body or cause stress in a fixed body. It can also be described by intuitive concepts such as a push or pull that can cause an object with mass to change its velocity, i.e., to accelerate, or which can cause a flexible object to deform. Force has both magnitude and direction, making it a vector quantity.

Froude number

The Froude number is a dimensionless number comparing inertia and gravitational forces. It may be used to quantify the resistance of an object moving through water, and compare objects of different sizes. Named after William Froude, the Froude number is based on his speed/length ratio.

Reynolds number

In fluid mechanics, the Reynolds number Re is a dimensionless number that gives a measure of the ratio of inertial forces (ρV^2) to viscous forces $\left(\frac{\mu V}{L}\right)$ and consequently quantifies the relative importance of these two types of forces for given flow conditions. The Reynolds number is named after Osborne Reynolds (1842-1912), who introduced its use in 1883.

Reynolds numbers frequently arise when performing dimensional analysis of fluid dynamics problems, and as such can be used to determine dynamic similitude between different experimental cases. They are also used to characterize different flow regimes, such as laminar or turbulent flow: laminar flow occurs at low Reynolds numbers, where viscous forces are dominant, and is characterized by smooth, constant fluid motion, while turbulent flow occurs at high Reynolds numbers and is dominated by inertial forces, which tend to produce random eddies, vortices and other flow instabilities.

Strouhal number

In dimensional analysis, the Strouhal number is a dimensionless number describing oscillating flow mechanisms. The parameter is named after Vincenc Strouhal, a Czech physicist who experimented in 1878 with wires experiencing vortex shedding and singing in the wind. The Strouhal number is an integral part of the fundamentals of fluid mechanics.

Chapter 7. SIMILITUDE, DIMENSIONAL ANALYSIS, AND MODELING

Chapter 7. SIMILITUDE, DIMENSIONAL ANALYSIS, AND MODELING

Weber number	The Weber number is a dimensionless number in fluid mechanics that is often useful in analysing fluid flows where there is an interface between two different fluids, especially for multiphase flows with strongly curved surfaces. It can be thought of as a measure of the relative importance of the fluid"s inertia compared to its surface tension. The quantity is useful in analyzing thin film flows and the formation of droplets and bubbles. It is named after Moritz Weber (1871-1951) and may be written as: $$We = \frac{\rho v^2 l}{\sigma}$$ where · ρ is the density of the fluid. · v is its velocity. · l is its characteristic length, typically the droplet diameter. · σ is the surface tension.
Compressibility	Compressibility is used in the Earth sciences to quantify the ability of a soil or rock to reduce in volume with applied pressure. This concept is important for specific storage, when estimating groundwater reserves in confined aquifers. Geologic materials are made up of two portions: solids and voids (or same as porosity).
Inertia	Inertia is the resistance of any physical object to a change in its state of motion. It is represented numerically by an object"s mass. The principle of Inertia is one of the fundamental principles of classical physics which are used to describe the motion of matter and how it is affected by applied forces.
Blasius	Paul Richard Heinrich Blasius (1883 - 1970) was a German fluid dynamics engineer. He was one of the first students of Prandtl who provided a mathematical basis for boundary-layer drag but also showed as early as 1911 that the resistance to flow through smooth pipes could be expressed in terms of the Reynolds number for both laminar and turbulent flow. One of his most notable contributions involves a description of the steady two-dimensional boundary-layer that forms on a semi-infinite plate which is held parallel to a constant unidirectional flow U.
Vector	In elementary mathematics, physics, and engineering, a vector is a geometric object that has both a magnitude (or length) and direction. A vector is frequently represented by a line segment with a definite direction, or graphically as an arrow, connecting an initial point A with a terminal point B, and denoted by $\overrightarrow{AB}$. A vector is what is needed to "carry" the point A to the point B; the Latin word vector means "one who carries". The magnitude of the vector is the distance between the two points and the direction refers to the direction of displacement from A to B. Many algebraic operations on real numbers such as addition, subtraction, multiplication, and negation have close analogues fs, operations which obey the familiar algebraic laws of commutativity, associativity, and distributivity.

Chapter 7. SIMILITUDE, DIMENSIONAL ANALYSIS, AND MODELING

Chapter 7. SIMILITUDE, DIMENSIONAL ANALYSIS, AND MODELING

Length scale | In physics, Length scale is a particular length or distance determined with the precision of one order (or a few orders) of magnitude. The concept of Length scale is particularly important because physical phenomena of different Length scales cannot affect each other and are said to decouple. The decoupling of different Length scales makes it possible to have a self-consistent theory that only describes the relevant Length scales for a given problem.

Drag coefficient | In fluid dynamics, the drag coefficient (commonly denoted as C_d, C_x or C_w) is a dimensionless quantity that is used to quantify the drag or resistance of an object in a fluid environment such as air or water. It is used in the drag equation, where a lower drag coefficient indicates the object will have less aerodynamic or hydrodynamic drag. The drag coefficient is always associated with a particular surface area.

Surface tension | Surface tension is a property of the surface of a liquid. It is what causes the surface portion of liquid to be attracted to another surface, such as that of another portion of liquid (as in connecting bits of water or as in a drop of mercury that forms a cohesive ball).
Applying Newtonian physics to the forces that arise due to Surface tension accurately predicts many liquid behaviors that are so commonplace that most people take them for granted.

Chapter 7. SIMILITUDE, DIMENSIONAL ANALYSIS, AND MODELING

Chapter 8. VISCOUS FLOW IN PIPES

Pipe flow

Pipe flow is subset of rheology.
It can roughly be divided into two:

· Laminar flow - see Hagen-Poiseuille flow
· Turbulent flow - see Moody diagram
The transition between the two is when the Reynolds number is approximately 2300.

Boundary layer

In physics and fluid mechanics, a Boundary layer is that layer of fluid in the immediate vicinity of a bounding surface. In the Earth"s atmosphere, the planetary Boundary layer is the air layer near the ground affected by diurnal heat, moisture or momentum transfer to or from the surface. On an aircraft wing the Boundary layer is the part of the flow close to the wing.

Vector

In elementary mathematics, physics, and engineering, a vector is a geometric object that has both a magnitude (or length) and direction. A vector is frequently represented by a line segment with a definite direction, or graphically as an arrow, connecting an initial point A with a terminal point B, and denoted by $\overrightarrow{AB}$.

A vector is what is needed to "carry" the point A to the point B; the Latin word vector means "one who carries". The magnitude of the vector is the distance between the two points and the direction refers to the direction of displacement from A to B. Many algebraic operations on real numbers such as addition, subtraction, multiplication, and negation have close analogues fs, operations which obey the familiar algebraic laws of commutativity, associativity, and distributivity.

Cylinder

A cylinder is one of the most basic curvilinear geometric shapes, the surface formed by the points at a fixed distance from a given straight line, the axis of the cylinder. The solid enclosed by this surface and by two planes perpendicular to the axis is also called a cylinder. The surface area and the volume of a cylinder have been known since deep antiquity.

Shearing

Shearing in continuum mechanics refers to the occurrence of a shear strain, which is a deformation of a material substance in which parallel internal surfaces slide past one another. It is induced by a shear stress in the material. Shear strain is distinguished from volumetric strain, the change in a material"s volume in response to stress.

Shear stress

A Shear stress, τ is applied to the top of the square while the bottom is held in place. This stress results in a strain, or deformation, changing the square into a parallelogram.
A Shear stress, denoted τ (tau), is defined as a stress which is applied parallel or tangential to a face of a material, as opposed to a normal stress which is applied perpendicularly.
The formula to calculate average Shear stress is:

$$\tau = \frac{F}{A}$$

where
τ = the Shear stress

Chapter 8. VISCOUS FLOW IN PIPES

Chapter 8. VISCOUS FLOW IN PIPES

F = the force applied
A = the cross sectional area
Beam shear is defined as the internal Shear stress of a beam caused by the shear force applied to the beam.

Velocity

In physics, velocity is the rate of change of position. It is a vector physical quantity; both speed and direction are required to define it. In the SI (metric) system, it is measured in meters per second: (m/s) or ms^{-1}.

Eddy

In fluid dynamics, an eddy is the swirling of a fluid and the reverse current created when the fluid flows past an obstacle. The moving fluid creates a space devoid of downstream-flowing fluid on the downstream side of the object. Fluid behind the obstacle flows into the void creating a swirl of fluid on each edge of the obstacle, followed by a short reverse flow of fluid behind the obstacle flowing upstream, toward the back of the obstacle.

Viscosity

Viscosity is a measure of the resistance of a fluid which is being deformed by either shear stress or extensional stress. In everyday terms (and for fluids only), Viscosity is "thickness." Thus, water is "thin," having a lower Viscosity, while honey is "thick," having a higher Viscosity. Viscosity describes a fluid"s internal resistance to flow and may be thought of as a measure of fluid friction.

Power

In physics, power is the rate at which work is performed or energy is converted. It is an energy per unit of time. As a rate of change of work done or the energy of a subsystem, power is

$$P = \frac{W}{t}$$

where P is power, W is work and t is time.

Flow velocity

In fluid dynamics the Flow velocity, of a fluid is a vector field which is used to mathematically describe the motion of a fluid. The length of the Flow velocity vector is the flow speed.
The Flow velocity u of a fluid is a vector field

$$\mathbf{u} = \mathbf{u}(\mathbf{x}, t)$$

which gives the velocity of an element of fluid at a position $\mathbf{x}$ and time t.

Fundamental diagram of traffic flow

The fundamental diagram of traffic flow is a diagram that gives a relation between the traffic flux (cars/hour) and the traffic density (cars/km). A macroscopic traffic model involving traffic flux, traffic density and velocity forms the basis of the fundamental diagram. It can be used to predict the capability of a road system, or its behaviour when applying inflow regulation or speed limits. fundamental diagram of traffic flow

Chapter 8. VISCOUS FLOW IN PIPES

Chapter 8. VISCOUS FLOW IN PIPES

· There is a connection between traffic density and vehicle velocity: The more vehicles are on a road, the slower their velocity will be.
· To prevent congestion and to keep traffic flow stable, the number of vehicles entering the control zone has to be smaller or equal to the number of vehicles leaving the zone in the same time.
· At a critical traffic density and a corresponding critical velocity the state of flow will change from stable to unstable.
· If one of the vehicles brakes in unstable flow regime the flow will collapse.

Maxima

In mathematics, maxima and minima, known collectively as extrema (singular: extremum), are the largest value (maximum) or smallest value (minimum), that a function takes in a point either within a given neighbourhood (local extremum) or on the function domain in its entirety (global extremum). More generally, the maxima and minima of a set (as defined in in set theory) are the greatest and least values in the set.

A real-valued function f defined on a real line is said to have a local (or relative) maximum point at the point x^*, if there exists some $\varepsilon > 0$ such that $f(x^*) \geq f(x)$ when $|x - x^*| < \varepsilon$.

Friction

Friction is the force resisting the relative lateral (tangential) motion of solid surfaces, fluid layers, and kinetic Friction (sometimes called sliding Friction or dynamic Friction) between moving surfaces.

· Lubricated Friction or fluid Friction resists relative lateral motion of two solid surfaces separated by a layer of gas or liquid.

· Fluid Friction is also used to describe the Friction between layers within a fluid that are moving relative to each other.

· Skin Friction is a component of drag, the force resisting the motion of a solid body through a fluid.

· Internal Friction is the force resisting motion between the elements making up a solid material while it undergoes deformation.

Friction is not a fundamental force, as it is derived from electromagnetic force between charged particles, including electrons, protons, atoms, and molecules, and so cannot be calculated from first principles, but instead must be found empirically.

Moody chart

The Moody chart is a graph in non-dimensional form that relates the friction factor, Reynolds number and relative roughness for fully developed flow in a circular pipe. It can be used for working out pressure drop or flow rate down such a pipe.

This dimensionless chart is used to work out pressure drop, ΔP (Pa) (or head loss, h_f (m)) and flow rate through pipes.

Chapter 8. VISCOUS FLOW IN PIPES

Chapter 8. VISCOUS FLOW IN PIPES

Hydraulic head

Hydraulic head or piezometric head is a specific measurement of water pressure above a geodetic datum. It is usually measured as a water surface elevation, expressed in units of length, at the entrance (or bottom) of a piezometer. In an aquifer, it can be calculated from the depth to water in a piezometric well (a specialized water well), and given information of the piezometer"s elevation and screen depth.

Blasius

Paul Richard Heinrich Blasius (1883 - 1970) was a German fluid dynamics engineer.
He was one of the first students of Prandtl who provided a mathematical basis for boundary-layer drag but also showed as early as 1911 that the resistance to flow through smooth pipes could be expressed in terms of the Reynolds number for both laminar and turbulent flow.
One of his most notable contributions involves a description of the steady two-dimensional boundary-layer that forms on a semi-infinite plate which is held parallel to a constant unidirectional flow U.

Reentrant

Reentrant or re-entrant can refer to:

· reentrant (subroutine) in computer coding.
· reentrant mutex in computer science.
· Salients, re-entrants and pockets in military tactics.
· reentrant tuning in music. .

Hydraulic

The word "hydraulics" originates from the Greek word á½'δραυλικÏŒες which in turn originates from á½•δραυλος (hydraulos) meaning water organ which in turn comes from á½•δωρ and αá½ λÏŒες .
The earliest masters of hydraulics in the Greek-Hellenized West were Ctesibius (flourished c. 270 BC) and Hero of Alexandria (c. 10-80 AD). Hero describes a number of working machines using hydraulic power, such as the force pump, which is known from many Roman sites as having been used for raising water and in fire engines, for example.

Hydraulic diameter

The Hydraulic diameter, D_H, is a commonly used term when handling flow in noncircular tubes and channels. Using this term one can calculate many things in the same way as for a round tube.
Definition:

$$D_H = \frac{4A}{P}$$

where A is the cross sectional area and P is the wetted perimeter of the cross-section.

Energy

Nuclear potential Energy, along with electric potential Energy, provides the Energy released from nuclear fission and nuclear fusion processes. The result of both these processes are nuclei in which the more-optimal size of the nucleus allows the nuclear force (which is opposed by the electromagnetic force) to bind nuclear particles more tightly together than before the reaction.
The Weak nuclear force provides the potential Energy for certain kinds of radioactive decay, such as beta decay.

Chapter 8. VISCOUS FLOW IN PIPES

Chapter 8. VISCOUS FLOW IN PIPES

Line	By defenition, a line is an infinite set of contiguous points in a plane that extend indefinitly in opposite directions such that the ratio of the verticle and horizontal displacements between any two points in the set is constant. In Euclidean geometry, a line is a straight curve. When geometry is used to model the real world, lines are used to represent straight objects with negligible width and height.
Nozzle	A Nozzle is a mechanical device designed to control the direction or characteristics of a fluid flow as it exits (or enters) an enclosed chamber or pipe via an orifice. A Nozzle is often a pipe or tube of varying cross sectional area, and it can be used to direct or modify the flow of a fluid (liquid or gas). Nozzles are frequently used to control the rate of flow, speed, direction, mass, shape, and/or the pressure of the stream that emerges from them.
Internality	An internality is a term used in behavioral economics to describe those types of behaviors that impose costs on a person in the long-run that are not taken into account when making decisions in the present. Classical Economics discourages government from creating legislation that targets internalities, because it is assumed that the consumer takes these personal costs into account when paying for the good that causes the internality. For example, cigarettes should be taxed because of the negative consumption externalities that they impose, such as second-hand smoke, not because the smoker harms him or herself by smoking.
Venturi effect	The Venturi effect is the reduction in fluid pressure that results when a fluid flows through a constricted section of pipe. The Venturi effect is named after Giovanni Battista Venturi, (1746-1822), an Italian physicist. The fluid velocity must increase through the constriction to satisfy the equation of continuity, while its pressure must decrease due to conservation of energy: the gain in kinetic energy is balanced by a drop in pressure or a pressure gradient force.

Chapter 8. VISCOUS FLOW IN PIPES

Chapter 9. FLOW OVER IMMERSED BODIES

External flow

In fluid mechanics, external flow is such a flow that boundary layers develop freely, without constraints imposed by adjacent surfaces. Accordingly, there will always exist a region of the flow outside the boundary layer in which velocity, temperature, and/or concentration gradients are negligible. It can be defined as the flow of a fluid around a body that is completely submerged in it.

An example includes fluid motion over a flat plate (inclined or parallel to the free stream velocity) and flow over curved surfaces such as a sphere, cylinder, airfoil, or turbine blade, air flowing around an airplane and water flowing around the submarines.

Wake

A Wake is the region of recirculating flow immediately behind a moving solid body, caused by the flow of surrounding fluid around the body.

In fluid dynamics, a Wake is the region of disturbed flow downstream of a solid body moving through a fluid, caused by the flow of the fluid around the body. In incompressible fluids (liquids) such as water, a bow Wake is created when a watercraft moves through the medium; as the medium cannot be compressed, it must be displaced instead, resulting in a wave.

Velocity

In physics, velocity is the rate of change of position. It is a vector physical quantity; both speed and direction are required to define it. In the SI (metric) system, it is measured in meters per second: (m/s) or ms^{-1}.

Force

In physics, a Force has the capacity to change the motion of a free body or cause stress in a fixed body. It can also be described by intuitive concepts such as a push or pull that can cause an object with mass to change its velocity, i.e., to accelerate, or which can cause a flexible object to deform. Force has both magnitude and direction, making it a vector quantity.

Lift

A fluid flowing past the surface of a body exerts a force on it. Lift is defined to be the component of this force that is perpendicular to the oncoming flow direction. It contrasts with the drag force, which is defined to be the component of the fluid-dynamic force parallel to the flow direction.

Pressure coefficient

The pressure coefficient is a dimensionless number which describes the relative pressures throughout a flow field in fluid dynamics. The pressure coefficient is used in aerodynamics and hydrodynamics. Every point in a fluid flow field has its own unique pressure coefficient, C_p.

Airfoil

An Airfoil or aerofoil is the shape of a wing or blade (of a propeller, rotor or turbine) or sail as seen in cross-section.

An Airfoil-shaped body moved through a fluid produces a force perpendicular to the motion called lift. Subsonic flight Airfoils have a characteristic shape with a rounded leading edge, followed by a sharp trailing edge, often with asymmetric camber.

Drag Force

In fluid dynamics, drag refers to forces that oppose the relative motion of an object through a fluid (a liquid or gas). Drag forces act in a direction opposite to the oncoming flow velocity. Unlike other resistive forces such as dry friction, which is nearly independent of velocity, Drag forces depend on velocity.

Chapter 9. FLOW OVER IMMERSED BODIES

Chapter 9. FLOW OVER IMMERSED BODIES

Drag coefficient

In fluid dynamics, the drag coefficient (commonly denoted as C_d, C_x or C_w) is a dimensionless quantity that is used to quantify the drag or resistance of an object in a fluid environment such as air or water. It is used in the drag equation, where a lower drag coefficient indicates the object will have less aerodynamic or hydrodynamic drag. The drag coefficient is always associated with a particular surface area.

Lift coefficient

The Lift coefficient (C_L or C_z) is a dimensionless coefficient that relates the lift generated by an airfoil, the dynamic pressure of the fluid flow around the airfoil, and the planform area of the airfoil. It may also be described as the ratio of lift pressure to dynamic pressure.

Lift coefficient may be used to relate the total lift generated by an aircraft to the total area of the wing of the aircraft. In this application it is called the aircraft Lift coefficient C_L.

The Lift coefficient C_L is equal to:

$$C_L = \frac{L}{\frac{1}{2}\rho v^2 A} = \frac{L}{qA}$$

where

- L is the lift force,
- ρ is fluid density,
- v is true airspeed,
- q is dynamic pressure, and
- A is planform area.

Reynolds number

In fluid mechanics, the Reynolds number Re is a dimensionless number that gives a measure of the ratio of inertial forces (ρV^2) to viscous forces $\left(\frac{\mu V}{L}\right)$ and consequently quantifies the relative importance of these two types of forces for given flow conditions. The Reynolds number is named after Osborne Reynolds (1842-1912), who introduced its use in 1883.

Reynolds numbers frequently arise when performing dimensional analysis of fluid dynamics problems, and as such can be used to determine dynamic similitude between different experimental cases. They are also used to characterize different flow regimes, such as laminar or turbulent flow: laminar flow occurs at low Reynolds numbers, where viscous forces are dominant, and is characterized by smooth, constant fluid motion, while turbulent flow occurs at high Reynolds numbers and is dominated by inertial forces, which tend to produce random eddies, vortices and other flow instabilities.

Flow network

In graph theory, a flow network is a directed graph where each edge has a capacity and each edge receives a flow. The amount of flow on an edge cannot exceed the capacity of the edge. Often in Operations Research, a directed graph is called a network, the vertices are called nodes and the edges are called arcs.

Chapter 9. FLOW OVER IMMERSED BODIES

Chapter 9. FLOW OVER IMMERSED BODIES

Cylinder

A cylinder is one of the most basic curvilinear geometric shapes, the surface formed by the points at a fixed distance from a given straight line, the axis of the cylinder. The solid enclosed by this surface and by two planes perpendicular to the axis is also called a cylinder. The surface area and the volume of a cylinder have been known since deep antiquity.

Blasius

Paul Richard Heinrich Blasius (1883 - 1970) was a German fluid dynamics engineer.
He was one of the first students of Prandtl who provided a mathematical basis for boundary-layer drag but also showed as early as 1911 that the resistance to flow through smooth pipes could be expressed in terms of the Reynolds number for both laminar and turbulent flow.
One of his most notable contributions involves a description of the steady two-dimensional boundary-layer that forms on a semi-infinite plate which is held parallel to a constant unidirectional flow U.

Boundary layer

In physics and fluid mechanics, a Boundary layer is that layer of fluid in the immediate vicinity of a bounding surface. In the Earth"s atmosphere, the planetary Boundary layer is the air layer near the ground affected by diurnal heat, moisture or momentum transfer to or from the surface. On an aircraft wing the Boundary layer is the part of the flow close to the wing.

Low pressure area

A low pressure area, is a region where the atmospheric pressure at sea level is lower in relation to surrounding locations. Low pressure systems form under areas wind divergence which occur in upper levels of the troposphere. Within the field of atmospheric dynamics, these areas of wind divergence aloft are either on the east side of upper troughs which form half of a Rossby wave within the Westerlies (a trough with large wavelength which extends through the troposphere), or ahead of embedded shortwave troughs which are of smaller wavelength.

Displacement thickness

Displacement thickness is the distance by which a surface would have to be moved parallel to itself towards the reference plane in an ideal fluid stream of velocity u_0 to give the same mass flow as occurs between the surface and the reference plane in a real fluid.
In practical aerodynamics, the displacement thickness essentially modifies the shape of a body immersed in a fluid. It is commonly used in aerodynamics to overcome the difficulty inherent in the fact that the fluid velocity in the boundary layer approaches asymptotically to the free stream value as distance from the wall increases at any given location.

Momentum

In classical mechanics, Momentum is the product of the mass and velocity of an object . For more accurate measures of Momentum, see the section "modern definitions of Momentum" on this page. It is sometimes referred to as linear Momentum to distinguish it from the related subject of angular Momentum.

Boundary layer thickness

In fluid dynamics, the boundary layer thickness (δ) is the distance from a fixed boundary wall where the flow velocity transitions from zero velocity at the wall (the no-slip condition) to the velocity of the free stream. Beyond δ the fluid is considered to move at a constant velocity. This distance is calculated based on the total momentum of the fluid, rather than the total mass, as in the case of displacement thickness (δ^*).

Chapter 9. FLOW OVER IMMERSED BODIES

Chapter 9. FLOW OVER IMMERSED BODIES

Shearing	Shearing in continuum mechanics refers to the occurrence of a shear strain, which is a deformation of a material substance in which parallel internal surfaces slide past one another. It is induced by a shear stress in the material. Shear strain is distinguished from volumetric strain, the change in a material"s volume in response to stress.
Stress	In linguistics, stress is the relative emphasis that may be given to certain syllables in a word. The term is also used for similar patterns of phonetic prominence inside syllables. The word accent is sometimes also used with this sense.
Friction	Friction is the force resisting the relative lateral (tangential) motion of solid surfaces, fluid layers, and kinetic Friction (sometimes called sliding Friction or dynamic Friction) between moving surfaces. · Lubricated Friction or fluid Friction resists relative lateral motion of two solid surfaces separated by a layer of gas or liquid. · Fluid Friction is also used to describe the Friction between layers within a fluid that are moving relative to each other. · Skin Friction is a component of drag, the force resisting the motion of a solid body through a fluid. · Internal Friction is the force resisting motion between the elements making up a solid material while it undergoes deformation. Friction is not a fundamental force, as it is derived from electromagnetic force between charged particles, including electrons, protons, atoms, and molecules, and so cannot be calculated from first principles, but instead must be found empirically.
Pressure gradient	In atmospheric sciences (meteorology, climatology and related fields), the Pressure gradient (typically of air, more generally of any fluid) is a physical quantity that describes in which direction and at what rate the pressure changes the most rapidly around a particular location. The Pressure gradient is a dimensional quantity expressed in units of pressure per unit length. The SI unit is pascal per metre (Pa/m).
Parasitic drag	Parasitic drag is drag caused by moving a solid object through a fluid medium (in the case of aerodynamics, more specifically, a gaseous medium). Parasitic drag is made up of many components, the most prominent being form drag. Skin friction and interference drag are also major components of Parasitic drag.
Nozzle	A Nozzle is a mechanical device designed to control the direction or characteristics of a fluid flow as it exits (or enters) an enclosed chamber or pipe via an orifice. A Nozzle is often a pipe or tube of varying cross sectional area, and it can be used to direct or modify the flow of a fluid (liquid or gas). Nozzles are frequently used to control the rate of flow, speed, direction, mass, shape, and/or the pressure of the stream that emerges from them.

Chapter 9. FLOW OVER IMMERSED BODIES

Chapter 9. FLOW OVER IMMERSED BODIES

Compressible flow	Compressible fluid mechanics is a combination of the fields of traditional fluid mechanics and thermodynamics. It is related to the more general study of compressibility. In fluid dynamics, a flow is considered to be a Compressible flow if the density of the fluid changes with respect to pressure.
Compressibility	Compressibility is used in the Earth sciences to quantify the ability of a soil or rock to reduce in volume with applied pressure. This concept is important for specific storage, when estimating groundwater reserves in confined aquifers. Geologic materials are made up of two portions: solids and voids (or same as porosity).
Shock wave	Schlieren photograph of an attached shock on a sharp-nosed supersonic body. A shock wave (also called shock front or simply "shock") is a type of propagating disturbance. Like an ordinary wave, it carries energy and can propagate through a medium (solid, liquid, gas or plasma) or in some cases in the absence of a material medium, through a field such as the electromagnetic field. shock waves are characterized by an abrupt, nearly discontinuous change in the characteristics of the medium.
Froude number	The Froude number is a dimensionless number comparing inertia and gravitational forces. It may be used to quantify the resistance of an object moving through water, and compare objects of different sizes. Named after William Froude, the Froude number is based on his speed/length ratio.
Angle of attack	Angle of attack is a term used in fluid dynamics to describe the angle between a reference line on a lifting body and the vector representing the relative motion between the lifting body and the fluid through which it is moving. Angle of attack is the angle between the lifting body"s reference line and the oncoming flow. In aviation, Angle of attack is used to describe the angle between the chord line of the wing of a fixed-wing aircraft and the vector representing the relative motion between the aircraft and the atmosphere.
Radiation pattern	In the field of antenna design the term "radiation pattern" most commonly refers to the directional (angular) dependence of radiation from the antenna or other source . Particularly in the fields of fiber optics, lasers, and integrated optics, the term radiation pattern, or near-field radiation pattern, may also be used as a synonym for the near-field pattern or Fresnel pattern. This refers to the positional dependence of the electromagnetic field in the near-field, or Fresnel region of the source.
Wing	A wing is an appendage used for flight by an animal or an apparatus used to create lift in aeronautics. wing s may also refer to: · Insect wing · Bat wing · Bird wing · wing (air force unit) · "wings", a colloquial term for the Aircrew Badge (US) or Aircrew brevet (UK) worn by military fliers and the Parachutist Badge worn by paratroopers

Chapter 9. FLOW OVER IMMERSED BODIES

Chapter 9. FLOW OVER IMMERSED BODIES

- wing, Buckinghamshire, a village in England
- wing, Rutland, a village in England
- Port wing (town), Wisconsin, a town (civil township) in the United States
- wing, North Dakota, a city in the United States
- wing River Township, Minnesota, a township in the United States

- wing (Transformers), a fictional character.
- Craig wing, a rugby league player for the Sydney Roosters
- Grace Barnett wing, birthname of Grace Slick, American lead singer of Jefferson Airplane and related acts
- Joseph wing and William Ricketson wing, owners of J. ' W. R. wing Company, a whaling company
- Lorna wing, a researcher of Asperger"s Syndrome
- Toby wing, an American actress
- wing (singer), a New Zealand singer originally from Hong Kong
- wings Hauser, an American actor

- wings (Aprilynne Pike), a young-adult faerie novel by Aprilynne Pike
- wing (DC Comics), a DC Comics character
- wing (Marvel Comics), a minor Astonishing X-Men character
- wings, by Mikhail Kuzmin
- wings (manga magazine)
- wings (play), a 1978 Arthur Kopit play
- wings, the third in The Bromeliad trilogy of children"s books by Terry Pratchett
- wing, an island in Julie Bertgna"s book Exodus (2002 novel)

- "wing" (South Park), an episode of South Park featuring the singer wing
- wings (TV series), which ran on NBC from 1990 to 1997
- wings (BBC TV series), a BBC drama which ran from 1976 to 1977
- wings (Discovery Channel TV series), documentary show about aircraft

- wings (band), Paul McCartney"s 1970s band
- wings (1968 band), an American folk rock band
- wings (Mark Chesnutt album), a 1995 album
- wings (Bonnie Tyler album), a 2005 album by singer Bonnie Tyler
- wing Records, a record label

- wings (film), a 1927 film about World War I fighter pilots
- wings (1966 film), by Soviet filmmaker Larisa Shepitko

Chapter 9. FLOW OVER IMMERSED BODIES

Chapter 9. FLOW OVER IMMERSED BODIES

- Detroit Red wings, an NHL hockey team
- Philadelphia wings, an NLL lacrosse team
- Kalamazoo wings, a UHL hockey team based in Kalamazoo, Michigan
- winger (sport), a position in several sports

- wings (1996 video game), a computer game with space ships
- wings (series), several World War I computer flying games by Cinemaware

- wing, a Windows interface in computing
- wings 3D, an open source computer graphics modeling program
- wings, a Widget toolkit used by Window Maker
- wings Display Manager, an X display manager

- airfoil or aerofoil, shape of a wing or blade or sail as seen in cross-section.
- T-Mobile wing, a Pocket PC telephone
- wings, or Backplate and wing, a type of buoyancy compensation device worn by scuba divers
- wings (haircut), a haircut style
- wings Alliance, a proposed airline alliance
- Fender (automobile) or wing, the automobile panel which surrounds the wheel
- wing, an AM radio station in Dayton, Ohio
- The wings, an area of a theatre stage, hidden from the audience
- wingS, an international camp organized by Girlguiding Royal Berkshire and Berkshire Scouts "

Wing loading

In aerodynamics, Wing loading is the loaded weight of the aircraft divided by the area of the wing. The faster an aircraft flies, the more lift is produced by each unit area of wing, so a smaller wing can carry the same weight in level flight, operating at a higher Wing loading. Correspondingly, the landing and take-off speeds will be higher.

Vector

In elementary mathematics, physics, and engineering, a vector is a geometric object that has both a magnitude (or length) and direction. A vector is frequently represented by a line segment with a definite direction, or graphically as an arrow, connecting an initial point A with a terminal point B, and denoted by $\overrightarrow{AB}$.

A vector is what is needed to "carry" the point A to the point B; the Latin word vector means "one who carries". The magnitude of the vector is the distance between the two points and the direction refers to the direction of displacement from A to B. Many algebraic operations on real numbers such as addition, subtraction, multiplication, and negation have close analogues fs, operations which obey the familiar algebraic laws of commutativity, associativity, and distributivity.

Chapter 9. FLOW OVER IMMERSED BODIES

Chapter 10. OPEN-CHANNEL FLOW

Supercritical flow	A supercritical flow is when the flow velocity is larger than the wave velocity. The analogous condition in gas dynamics is supersonic. Information travels at the wave velocity.
Surface wave	In physics, a Surface wave is a mechanical wave that propagates along the interface between differing media, usually two fluids with different densities. A Surface wave can also be an electromagnetic wave guided by a refractive index gradient. In radio transmission, a ground wave is a Surface wave that propagates close to the surface of the Earth.
Froude number	The Froude number is a dimensionless number comparing inertia and gravitational forces. It may be used to quantify the resistance of an object moving through water, and compare objects of different sizes. Named after William Froude, the Froude number is based on his speed/length ratio.
Vector	In elementary mathematics, physics, and engineering, a vector is a geometric object that has both a magnitude (or length) and direction. A vector is frequently represented by a line segment with a definite direction, or graphically as an arrow, connecting an initial point A with a terminal point B, and denoted by $\overrightarrow{AB}$. A vector is what is needed to "carry" the point A to the point B; the Latin word vector means "one who carries". The magnitude of the vector is the distance between the two points and the direction refers to the direction of displacement from A to B. Many algebraic operations on real numbers such as addition, subtraction, multiplication, and negation have close analogues fs, operations which obey the familiar algebraic laws of commutativity, associativity, and distributivity.
Vortex ring toy	A Vortex ring toy generates vortex rings -- rolling donut-shapes of fluid -- which move through the fluid (most often air, and). A smoke ring is a common example of a vortex ring. Because of the way they rotate, a vortex ring can hold itself together and travel for quite a distance.
Energy	Nuclear potential Energy, along with electric potential Energy, provides the Energy released from nuclear fission and nuclear fusion processes. The result of both these processes are nuclei in which the more-optimal size of the nucleus allows the nuclear force (which is opposed by the electromagnetic force) to bind nuclear particles more tightly together than before the reaction. The Weak nuclear force provides the potential Energy for certain kinds of radioactive decay, such as beta decay.
Line	By defenition, a line is an infinite set of contiguous points in a plane that extend indefinitly in opposite directions such that the ratio of the verticle and horizontal displacements between any two points in the set is constant. In Euclidean geometry, a line is a straight curve. When geometry is used to model the real world, lines are used to represent straight objects with negligible width and height.
Friction	Friction is the force resisting the relative lateral (tangential) motion of solid surfaces, fluid layers, and kinetic Friction (sometimes called sliding Friction or dynamic Friction) between moving surfaces. · Lubricated Friction or fluid Friction resists relative lateral motion of two solid surfaces separated by a layer of gas or liquid.

Chapter 10. OPEN-CHANNEL FLOW

Chapter 10. OPEN-CHANNEL FLOW

· Fluid Friction is also used to describe the Friction between layers within a fluid that are moving relative to each other.

· Skin Friction is a component of drag, the force resisting the motion of a solid body through a fluid.

· Internal Friction is the force resisting motion between the elements making up a solid material while it undergoes deformation.

Friction is not a fundamental force, as it is derived from electromagnetic force between charged particles, including electrons, protons, atoms, and molecules, and so cannot be calculated from first principles, but instead must be found empirically.

Shearing

Shearing in continuum mechanics refers to the occurrence of a shear strain, which is a deformation of a material substance in which parallel internal surfaces slide past one another. It is induced by a shear stress in the material. Shear strain is distinguished from volumetric strain, the change in a material"s volume in response to stress.

Stress

In linguistics, stress is the relative emphasis that may be given to certain syllables in a word. The term is also used for similar patterns of phonetic prominence inside syllables. The word accent is sometimes also used with this sense.

Hydraulic

The word "hydraulics" originates from the Greek word á½'δραυλικϊŒς which in turn originates from á½·δραυλος (hydraulos) meaning water organ which in turn comes from á½·δωρ and αá½½ λϊŒς . The earliest masters of hydraulics in the Greek-Hellenized West were Ctesibius (flourished c. 270 BC) and Hero of Alexandria (c. 10-80 AD). Hero describes a number of working machines using hydraulic power, such as the force pump, which is known from many Roman sites as having been used for raising water and in fire engines, for example.

Manning formula

The Manning formula, known also as the Gauckler-Manning formula, is an empirical formula for open channel flow, or free-surface flow driven by gravity. It was first presented by the French engineer Philippe Gauckler in 1867, and later re-developed by the Irish engineer Robert Manning in 1890. The Gauckler-Manning formula states:

$$V = \frac{k}{n} R_h^{\frac{2}{3}} \cdot S^{\frac{1}{2}}$$

where:

The discharge formula, Q = A V, can be used to manipulate Gauckler-Manning"s equation by substitution for V. Solving for Q then allows an estimate of the volumetric flow rate (discharge) without knowing the limiting or actual flow velocity.

The Gauckler-Manning formula is used to estimate flow in open channel situations where it is not practical to construct a weir or flume to measure flow with greater accuracy.

Chapter 10. OPEN-CHANNEL FLOW

Chapter 10. OPEN-CHANNEL FLOW

Shear stress

A Shear stress, $\mathcal{T}$ is applied to the top of the square while the bottom is held in place. This stress results in a strain, or deformation, changing the square into a parallelogram.

A Shear stress, denoted $\mathcal{T}$ (tau), is defined as a stress which is applied parallel or tangential to a face of a material, as opposed to a normal stress which is applied perpendicularly.

The formula to calculate average Shear stress is:

$$\tau = \frac{F}{A}$$

where

τ = the Shear stress

F = the force applied

A = the cross sectional area

Beam shear is defined as the internal Shear stress of a beam caused by the shear force applied to the beam.

Hydraulic jump

A hydraulic jump is a phenomenon in the science of hydraulics which is frequently observed in open channel flow such as rivers and spillways. When liquid at high velocity discharges into a zone of lower velocity, a rather abrupt rise (a step or standing wave) occurs in the liquid surface. The rapidly flowing liquid is abruptly slowed and increases in height converting some of the flow"s initial kinetic energy into an increase in potential energy, with some energy irreversibly lost through turbulence to heat.

Hydraulic head

Hydraulic head or piezometric head is a specific measurement of water pressure above a geodetic datum. It is usually measured as a water surface elevation, expressed in units of length, at the entrance (or bottom) of a piezometer. In an aquifer, it can be calculated from the depth to water in a piezometric well (a specialized water well), and given information of the piezometer"s elevation and screen depth.

Venturi effect

The Venturi effect is the reduction in fluid pressure that results when a fluid flows through a constricted section of pipe. The Venturi effect is named after Giovanni Battista Venturi, (1746-1822), an Italian physicist.

The fluid velocity must increase through the constriction to satisfy the equation of continuity, while its pressure must decrease due to conservation of energy: the gain in kinetic energy is balanced by a drop in pressure or a pressure gradient force.

Drop structure

A Drop structure, also known as a grade control, sill, is a manmade structure, typically small and built on minor streams, to pass water to a lower elevation while controlling the energy and velocity of the water as it passes over. Unlike weirs and dams, Drop structures are usually not built for water impoundment, diversion or raising the water level. Mostly built on streams and rivers with steep channel gradients, they serve the other purposes of water oxygenation and erosion prevention.

Nozzle

A Nozzle is a mechanical device designed to control the direction or characteristics of a fluid flow as it exits (or enters) an enclosed chamber or pipe via an orifice.

Chapter 10. OPEN-CHANNEL FLOW

Chapter 10. OPEN-CHANNEL FLOW

A Nozzle is often a pipe or tube of varying cross sectional area, and it can be used to direct or modify the flow of a fluid (liquid or gas). Nozzles are frequently used to control the rate of flow, speed, direction, mass, shape, and/or the pressure of the stream that emerges from them.

Chapter 10. OPEN-CHANNEL FLOW

Chapter 11. TURBOMACHINES

Machine	A machine is any device that uses energy to perform some activity. In common usage, the meaning is that of a device having parts that perform or assist in performing any type of work. A simple machine is a device that transforms the direction or magnitude of a force without consuming any energy.
Axial compressors	Axial compressors are rotating, airfoil based compressors in which the working fluid principally flows parallel to the axis of rotation. This is in contrast with other rotating compressors such as centrifugal, axi-centrifugal and mixed-flow compressors where the air may enter axially but will have a significant radial component on exit. Axial flow compressors produce a continuous flow of compressed gas, and have the benefits of high efficiencies and large mass flow capacity, particularly in relation to their cross-section.
Hydraulic head	Hydraulic head or piezometric head is a specific measurement of water pressure above a geodetic datum. It is usually measured as a water surface elevation, expressed in units of length, at the entrance (or bottom) of a piezometer. In an aquifer, it can be calculated from the depth to water in a piezometric well (a specialized water well), and given information of the piezometer''s elevation and screen depth.
Maxima	In mathematics, maxima and minima, known collectively as extrema (singular: extremum), are the largest value (maximum) or smallest value (minimum), that a function takes in a point either within a given neighbourhood (local extremum) or on the function domain in its entirety (global extremum). More generally, the maxima and minima of a set (as defined in in set theory) are the greatest and least values in the set. A real-valued function f defined on a real line is said to have a local (or relative) maximum point at the point x^*, if there exists some $\varepsilon > 0$ such that $f(x^*) \geq f(x)$ when $|x - x^*| < \varepsilon$.
Relative velocity	In kinematics, Relative velocity is the vector difference between the velocities of two objects, as evaluated in terms of a single coordinate system, usually an inertial frame of reference unless specifically stated otherwise. For example, if the velocities of particles A and B are $\mathbf{V}_A$ and $\mathbf{V}_B$ respectively in terms of a given inertial coordinate system, then the Relative velocity of A with respect to B (also called the velocity of A relative to B, or $\mathbf{V}_{A\ rel\ B}$) is $\mathbf{V}_{A\ rel\ B} = \mathbf{V}_A - \mathbf{V}_B$. Conversely, the velocity of B relative to A is $\mathbf{V}_{B\ rel\ A} = \mathbf{V}_B - \mathbf{V}_A$.
Velocity	In physics, velocity is the rate of change of position. It is a vector physical quantity; both speed and direction are required to define it. In the SI (metric) system, it is measured in meters per second: (m/s) or ms^{-1}.
Momentum	In classical mechanics, Momentum is the product of the mass and velocity of an object. For more accurate measures of Momentum, see the section "modern definitions of Momentum" on this page. It is sometimes referred to as linear Momentum to distinguish it from the related subject of angular Momentum.

Chapter 11. TURBOMACHINES

Chapter 11. TURBOMACHINES

Power

In physics, power is the rate at which work is performed or energy is converted. It is an energy per unit of time. As a rate of change of work done or the energy of a subsystem, power is

$$P = \frac{W}{t}$$

where P is power, W is work and t is time.

Torque

Torque,), is the tendency of a force to rotate an object about an axis, fulcrum, or pivot. Just as a force is a push or a pull, a Torque can be thought of as a twist.
In more basic terms, Torque measures how hard something is rotated.

Centrifugal pump

A Centrifugal pump is a rotodynamic pump that uses a rotating impeller to increase the pressure of a fluid. Centrifugal pumps are commonly used to move liquids through a piping system. The fluid enters the pump impeller along or near to the rotating axis and is accelerated by the impeller, flowing radially outward into a diffuser or volute chamber (casing), from where it exits into the downstream piping system.

Eye

Eyes are organs that detect light, and send electrical impulses along the optic nerve to the visual and other areas of the brain. Complex optical systems with resolving power have come in ten fundamentally different forms, and 96% of animal species possess a complex optical system. Image-resolving Eyes are present in cnidaria, molluscs, chordates, annelids and arthropods.

Impeller

An Impeller is a rotor inside a tube or conduit to increase the pressure and flow of a fluid. An Impeller for a dam turbine generator Several different types of pump Impellers
An Impeller is a rotating component of a centrifugal pump, usually made of iron, steel, bronze, brass, aluminum or plastic, which transfers energy from the motor that drives the pump to the fluid being pumped by accelerating the fluid outwards from the center of rotation. The velocity achieved by the Impeller transfers into pressure when the outward movement of the fluid is confined by the pump casing.

Flow coefficient

The Flow coefficient of a device is a relative measure of its efficiency at allowing fluid flow. It describes the relationship between the pressure drop across an orifice, valve or other assembly and the corresponding flow rate.
Mathematically the Flow coefficient can be expressed as:

$$C_v = F\sqrt{\frac{SG}{\Delta P}}$$

where:
C_v = Flow coefficient or flow capacity rating of valve.
F = Rate of flow (US gallons per minute).
SG = Specific gravity of fluid (Water = 1).
ΔP = Pressure drop across valve (psi).

Stator

The Stator is the stationary part of a rotor system, such as in an electric generator or electric motor

Chapter 11. TURBOMACHINES

Chapter 11. TURBOMACHINES

Depending on the configuration of a spinning electromotive device the Stator may act as the field magnet, interacting with the armature to create motion, or it may act as the armature, receiving its influence from moving field coils on the rotor.

The first DC generators (known as dynamos) and DC motors put the field coils on the Stator, and the power generation or motive reaction coils on the rotor. This was necessary because a continuously moving power switch known as the commutator is needed to keep the field correctly aligned across the spinning rotor.

Impulse

Impulse I produced from time t_1 to t_2 is defined to be

$$\mathbf{I} = \int_{t_1}^{t_2} \mathbf{F}\, dt$$

where F is the force applied dt denotes an infinitesimal amount of time.
From Newton"s second law, force is related to momentum p by

$$\mathbf{F} = \frac{d\mathbf{p}}{dt}.$$

Therefore

$$\mathbf{I} = \int_{t_1}^{t_2} \frac{d\mathbf{p}}{dt}\, dt$$

$$= \int_{t_1}^{t_2} d\mathbf{p}$$

$$= \Delta \mathbf{p},$$

where Δp is the change in momentum from time t_1 to t_2. This is often called the Impulse-momentum theorem.

Compressible flow

Compressible fluid mechanics is a combination of the fields of traditional fluid mechanics and thermodynamics. It is related to the more general study of compressibility. In fluid dynamics, a flow is considered to be a Compressible flow if the density of the fluid changes with respect to pressure.

Fluid

A Fluid is a substance that continually deforms (flows) under an applied shear stress. All gases are Fluids, but not all liquids are Fluids. Fluids are a subset of the phases of matter and include liquids, gases, plasmas and, to some extent, plastic solids.

Grid method

The Grid method is a form of long multiplication using a Partial Products Algorithm. Traditional long multiplication of, for instance, 26 x 13, would be written like this:
26 13 -- 78260---338
Using the Grid method, 26 x 13 would look like this:
200 60 60 18---338

Chapter 11. TURBOMACHINES

Chapter 11. TURBOMACHINES

	The Grid method differs in clearly breaking the multiplication and addition into two steps, and in being less dependent on place value. In recent years it has become very common in primary schools in England.
Viscosity	Viscosity is a measure of the resistance of a fluid which is being deformed by either shear stress or extensional stress. In everyday terms (and for fluids only), Viscosity is "thickness." Thus, water is "thin," having a lower Viscosity, while honey is "thick," having a higher Viscosity. Viscosity describes a fluid"s internal resistance to flow and may be thought of as a measure of fluid friction.
Sound	Sound is a travelling wave which is an oscillation of pressure transmitted through a solid, liquid, composed of frequencies within the range of hearing and of a level sufficiently strong to be heard, or the sensation stimulated in organs of hearing by such vibrations. Human ear For humans, hearing is normally limited to frequencies between about 12 Hz and 20,000 Hz (20 kHz), although these limits are not definite. The upper limit generally decreases with age.
Vortex ring toy	A Vortex ring toy generates vortex rings -- rolling donut-shapes of fluid -- which move through the fluid (most often air, and). A smoke ring is a common example of a vortex ring. Because of the way they rotate, a vortex ring can hold itself together and travel for quite a distance.
Acoustic	Acoustic or sonic lubrication occurs when sound (measurable in a vacuum by placing a microphone on one element of the sliding system) permits vibration to introduce separation between the sliding faces. This could happen between two plates or between a series of particles. The frequency of sound required to induce optimal vibration, and thus cause sonic lubrication, varies with the size of the particles (high frequencies will have the desired, or undesired, effect on sand and lower frequencies will have this effect on boulders).
Density	The Density of a material is defined as its mass per unit volume. The symbol of Density is ρ . Mathematically: $$\rho = \frac{m}{V}$$ where: ρ is the Density, m is the mass, V is the volume.
Physical properties	A physical property is any aspect of an object or substance that can be measured or perceived without changing its identity. Physical properties can be intensive or extensive. An intensive property does not depend on the size or amount of matter in the object, while an extensive property does.
Surface tension	Surface tension is a property of the surface of a liquid. It is what causes the surface portion of liquid to be attracted to another surface, such as that of another portion of liquid (as in connecting bits of water or as in a drop of mercury that forms a cohesive ball).

Chapter 11. TURBOMACHINES

Chapter 11. TURBOMACHINES

	Applying Newtonian physics to the forces that arise due to Surface tension accurately predicts many liquid behaviors that are so commonplace that most people take them for granted.
Vapor	A vapor (American spelling) or vapour is a substance in the gas phase at a temperature lower than its critical temperature. This means that the vapor can be condensed to a liquid or to a solid by increasing its pressure, without reducing the temperature. For example, water has a critical temperature of 374°C (or 647 K) which is the highest temperature at which liquid water can exist.
Vapor pressure	Vapor pressure or equilibrium Vapor pressure is the pressure of a vapor in thermodynamic equilibrium with its condensed phases in a closed container. All liquids and solids have a tendency to evaporate into a gaseous form, and all gases have a tendency to condense back to their liquid or solid form. The equilibrium Vapor pressure is an indication of a liquid"s evaporation rate.
Vapour pressure of water	The vapour pressure of water is the vapour pressure (or equilibrium/saturation pressure) of water, i.e., the pressure exerted by water at a specific temperature. It is important in many experiments, particularly experiments relating to gases. A common classroom experiment in which the vapour pressure at various temperatures table is used is when trying to find the molar mass of butane.
Water Vapor	Water vapor or water vapour , also aqueous vapor, is the gas phase of water. water vapor is one state of the water cycle within the hydrosphere. water vapor can be produced from the evaporation or boiling of liquid water or from the sublimation of ice.
Acceleration	Acceleration is the rate of change of velocity. At any point on a trajectory, the magnitude of the Acceleration is given by the rate of change of velocity in both magnitude and direction at that point. The true Acceleration at time t is found in the limit as time interval $\Delta t \rightarrow 0$. Components of Acceleration for a planar curved motion.
Atmosphere	An Atmosphere is a layer of gases that may surround a material body of sufficient mass, by the gravity of the body, and are retained for a longer duration if gravity is high and the Atmosphere"s temperature is low. Some planets consist mainly of various gases, but only their outer layer is their Atmosphere . The term stellar Atmosphere describes the outer region of a star, and typically includes the portion starting from the opaque photosphere outwards.
Pressure coefficient	The pressure coefficient is a dimensionless number which describes the relative pressures throughout a flow field in fluid dynamics. The pressure coefficient is used in aerodynamics and hydrodynamics. Every point in a fluid flow field has its own unique pressure coefficient, C_p.
Airfoil	An Airfoil or aerofoil is the shape of a wing or blade (of a propeller, rotor or turbine) or sail as seen in cross-section.

Chapter 11. TURBOMACHINES

Chapter 11. TURBOMACHINES

	An Airfoil-shaped body moved through a fluid produces a force perpendicular to the motion called lift. Subsonic flight Airfoils have a characteristic shape with a rounded leading edge, followed by a sharp trailing edge, often with asymmetric camber.
Control volume	In fluid mechanics and thermodynamics, a Control volume is a mathematical abstraction employed in the process of creating mathematical models of physical processes. In an inertial frame of reference, it is a fixed volume in space through which the fluid (gas or liquid) flows. The surface enclosing the Control volume is referred to as the control surface.
Conservation of energy	The law of Conservation of energy is an empirical law of physics. It states that the total amount of energy in a closed system remains constant over time (are said to be conserved over time). A consequence of this law is that energy cannot be created nor destroyed.
Linear momentum	In classical mechanics, momentum is the product of the mass and velocity of an object. For more accurate measures of momentum, see the section "modern definitions of momentum" on this page. It is sometimes referred to as linear momentum to distinguish it from the related subject of angular momentum.
Cylinder	A cylinder is one of the most basic curvilinear geometric shapes, the surface formed by the points at a fixed distance from a given straight line, the axis of the cylinder. The solid enclosed by this surface and by two planes perpendicular to the axis is also called a cylinder. The surface area and the volume of a cylinder have been known since deep antiquity.
Mass	In physics, Mass commonly refers to any of three properties of matter, which have been shown experimentally to be equivalent: inertial Mass, active gravitational Mass and passive gravitational Mass. In everyday usage, Mass is often taken to mean weight, but care should be taken to distinguish between the two terms in scientific use, as they actually refer to different properties. The inertial Mass of an object determines its acceleration in the presence of an applied force.

Chapter 11. TURBOMACHINES

CPSIA information can be obtained
at www.ICGtesting.com
Printed in the USA
BVHW091113180720
583943BV00012B/238